LOST COUNTRY HOUSES OF THE WEST MIDLANDS

MAXWELL CRAVEN AND JAMES DARWIN

AMBERLEY

This edition first published 2026

Amberley Publishing
The Hill, Stroud
Gloucestershire GL5 4EP

www.amberley-books.com

British Library Cataloguing in Publication Data.
A catalogue record for this book is available from the British Library.

ISBN 978 1 3981 3120 0 (print)
ISBN 978 1 3981 3121 7 (ebook)

Origination by Amberley Publishing.
Printed in Great Britain.

Appointed GPSR EU Representative: Easy Access System Europe Oü, 16879218
Address: Mustamäe tee 50, 10621, Tallinn, Estonia
Contact Details: gpsr.requests@easproject.com, +358 40 500 3575

Acknowledgements

The authors stand in debt to a large number of people in the preparation of this book, not least, the kindness of Amberley Publishing and the helpfulness of Nick Grant in particular. They would like to most warmly acknowledge the assistance rendered by those responsible for the resources they have consulted, most especially of the Georgian Group, Birmingham Libraries and Archives, Wolverhampton Local History Library, Coventry Libraries, Staffordshire Record Office, the William Salt Library, English Heritage/Historic England, the National Monuments Record and a variety of local history and civic societies who have been invaluable, not to mention the wealth of knowledge published in the August pages of the Staffordshire Record Society.

Heartfelt thanks are also due to a number of friends and people willing to share their expertise, especially to James Cartland and Nicholas Kingsley, and also to others who are now no longer with us, notably Sir Howard Colvin, B. F. J. Pardoe and Edward Saunders, without whom this book would not have been remotely possible. Others who have kindly made illustrations available are acknowledged with the relevant picture, although some have chosen to remain anonymous. Every effort has been made to identify and contact the correct originators of photographs; where we have failed, the presence of the images testify to our gratitude.

The authors would also be most pleased to hear, too, from anyone who can throw further light upon any of the houses mentioned, or others omitted (this mainly due to the paucity of illustrations), or are able to offer corrections, for any mistakes are entirely our own, and in a work of this scope, impossible wholly to avoid.

Introduction

Sir Roy Strong, in his introduction to the catalogue of *The Destruction of the Country House* held at the Victoria and Albert Museum in 1974, wrote of the way that, in the British countryside, we then took for granted our country houses. 'Like our parish churches,' he wrote, 'the country houses seem always to have been there, since time immemorial part of the fabric of our heritage.' It would seem invidious to add that in 1974 we also took for granted the vicarage, the pub, the shop, the post office and the pleasure of sharing a stirrup cup with the meet on Boxing Day – all institutions, if anything, even more under threat today than the country house.

The losses of country houses in present-day West Midlands county during the twentieth century have been catastrophic, no less so than poor Staffordshire to the north and east. Indeed, this volume started out as one element of *The Lost Country Houses of Staffordshire* (Amberley 2026) until lost house overload decreed that we should treat the West Midlands separately. As it turned out, we could, given enough local pictures and photographs, have run *The Lost Houses of the West Midlands* to a second volume, too, such has been the destruction wrought on middle England by the spread of industry and the housing required to accompany it.

The West Midlands has fared so badly due to the rapid industrialisation of the area around Birmingham, Coventry, Wolverhampton and their adjacent towns. The abundance of coal, clay deposits and other natural resources was the *raison d'être* of this remorseless expansion, which, in the case of mining, gradually claimed many losses, from the expansion of the pits, the necessity of house workers, the march of railways and need for power; unexpected subsidence destabilised houses that were not even in the way. Nor did this deleterious tendency stop when the Industrial Revolution began to lose steam in the later twentieth century.

The county of the West Midlands, in the years since 1969, when listed building consent was first required prior to the demolition of the listed building (previously only notification to RCHM(E) was required) and 1974, when it came into being as a legislative entity, has seen four substantial houses lost. Yet in the years 1945 to 1968, no fewer than thirty-two (that are dealt with here – there were others) were destroyed, including important buildings like Ward End (1945) and Elmdon Halls (1948), Whitley (1953) and Warley Abbeys (1957) and The Ellowes (1964). Nevertheless, before that, the destruction had been even worse. The figures speak for themselves: in 1928, 1937, 1940 and 1948 each, three houses were lost, but by far the worst year was 1963, which saw the destruction of five: The Grove, Harborne, Barnhurst Old Hall, Kingstanding Manor, Oakwell Hall and Ellowes Hall. Hence, the 1968 Town and Country Planning Act and the 1974 V & A exhibition together were a significant watershed and indeed these figures repeat for most lowland counties – not that statutory designation ever put off a really determined local planning authority or a Secretary of State from granting consent for demolition.

Of course, those with even a little local knowledge would gladly point out that another *annus horribilis* for the country house in the area of the present West Midlands county was 1791. It was in the July of that year that a mob, fuelled by righteous indignation, rampaged through the environs of Birmingham torching the houses of the great and good, four of which are recorded here. At that period, Birmingham was undergoing its second great expansion of business and trade, driven by a largely interlinked group of Nonconformist entrepreneurs who, through being disenfranchised by much earlier legislation, turned from the pursuit of political or court appointments to business, success in which led to fiscal surpluses, which in turn were profitably and usefully ploughed into banking. These radical entrepreneurs had espoused American independence, the abolition of the slave trade and enthusiastically welcomed the French Revolution. As a coterie, they dominated Birmingham and their decision to hold a banquet in summer 1791 to celebrate the French Revolution sparked what was called the 'Church and King' riot: an example of a certain radical hubris causing undetected resentment amongst a largely disenfranchised wider population, an unintended consequence which might be seen to reverberate even today.

Yet for all this, country houses have for centuries been destroyed for a wide variety of reasons. The most common reason for the destruction of an important house before 1919 – apart from the random but ever-present threat of fire – was unusually the desire of the owner to improve the standard of his accommodation, or to expand it, often commensurate with a rise in status. In the nineteenth century, an agricultural boom, which lasted throughout the middle years until about 1873, coupled with a superfluity of labour, caused households to expand, and more and better standards of service accommodation was required. Some owners met these needs by enlarging, others by demolition and replacement. Other factors include the amalgamation of estates, war (especially the English Civil War), plague, urban expansion, trunk road widening, mining, lack of tenants, land requisition for infrastructure, financial pressure and taxation (Lloyd George's death duties especially), local authority neglect, philistinism and sheer bloody mindedness – persistent cause of destruction.

The demolition of houses, therefore, can be seen as a continuing process of loss and renewal until the twentieth century, when losses accelerated alarmingly and little in terms of renewal was on offer. A substantial and largely unsung portion of our cultural and artistic heritage was swept away in a swathe of destruction over some sixty-five years, 1919–74, when no fewer than sixty-three out of the county total of houses recorded in these pages were destroyed.

This book aims to give a brief written summary and visual record of the majority of the losses, as far as the available images permit, with brief descriptive and historical captions, and may be viewed as a locally complementary work to add fine detail to Giles Worsley's *The Lost Houses of Britain* (Aurum Press/Country Life, 2002), to Peter Reid's *Burke's and Savill's Guide to the Country of the West Midlands* (which covered, inter alia, Warwickshire and Worcestershire) and to Geoffrey Tyack's *Country Houses of Warwickshire*, to some of the former of which we are able to offer minor corrections.

The following entries are by date of demolition (occasionally approximate), rather than cause of loss or date of building; we have also added – as a reminder of the fact that the county of the West Midlands is a relatively recent construct comprised of large areas of three historic counties – the name of the relevant historic county after the title of each entry.

Maxwell Craven, James Darwin

1. Dudley Castle, Dudley, Staffordshire. 1750

Dudley was originally in Worcester. Its castle and Castle Hill, however, lay in the county of Stafford. The original (probably timber) castle was built in the eleventh century by William FitzAnsculf, from whom it came to Gervase de Pagenel before being largely demolished in 1173. Roger de Somery, however, was granted a licence to crenellate his house there in 1264 and his fortified manor house survived in the Sutton family and then in their cadet branch the Dudleys, until rebuilt extensively and lavishly in 1552–53 for John Dudley, Duke of Northumberland, for which John Chapman supplied a chimneypiece. It passed in 1621 to the Ward family (later Lords Dudley and Earls of Dudley), who held it for the king in the Civil War before it was surrendered to Sir William Brereton in May 1645 and slighted the following year. However, the domestic ranges survived and the Lords Dudley continued there until July 1750, when a serious fire destroyed the main ranges. The extensive ruins and 40 acres of former pleasure grounds were adapted in the 1937 by the 3rd Earl of Dudley as a zoo, with new buildings by Berthold Lubetkin. It was municipalised in 1977, vested in a charity the following year and access to the ruins comes with entry to the zoo.

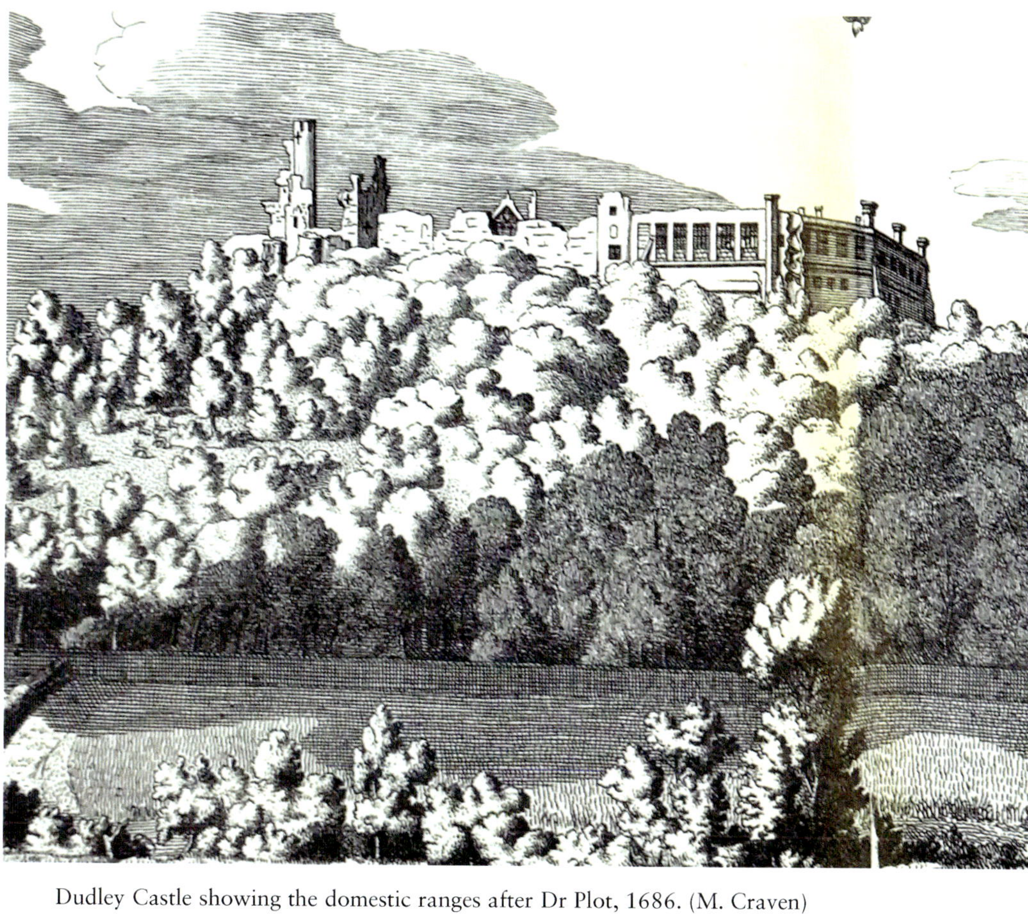

Dudley Castle showing the domestic ranges after Dr Plot, 1686. (M. Craven)

2. New House, Radford/Keresley, Coventry, Warwickshire. 1778

The estate, emparked in 1332, originated as part of monastic holdings and lay partly in Radford and part in both Keresley and Whitmore. It was acquired by Sir Ralph Sadler PC (1507–87) later to be the gaoler of Mary, Queen of Scots, in 1547, who granted it to fellow courtier John Hales, from whom it came in 1572 to his homonymous nephew. He built a substantial mansion of ashlar in 1586, named Hales Place, the slightly asymmetrical eight-bay façade of two storeys with attic gables being lit by mullioned and transomed windows and enclosed by a pair of octagonal turrets with ogee caps. On his death the house and its 436-acre park were sold to Sir Richard Burnaby, from whom it had come to Commons Speaker Sir Christopher Yelverton, who died in 1612. From the Yelvertons it descended to George Bohun, who in the 1680s added another eight-bay range to the north-east with attic dormers, cross windows and a tetrastyle Doric portico. His daughter and heiress, Susan, brought it to Gilbert Clarke of Chilcote (d. 1725), whose son Godfrey (1713–74) bought Sutton Scarsdale in Derbyshire and whose heir demolished the house in 1778. A later house on the by then 148-acre estate, Whitmore Hall, was enlarged by Abraham Barbery Herbert and rechristened Moat Hall. P. J. Muntz and Sidney Cash were later occupiers, but it succumbed to a housing development in 1929.

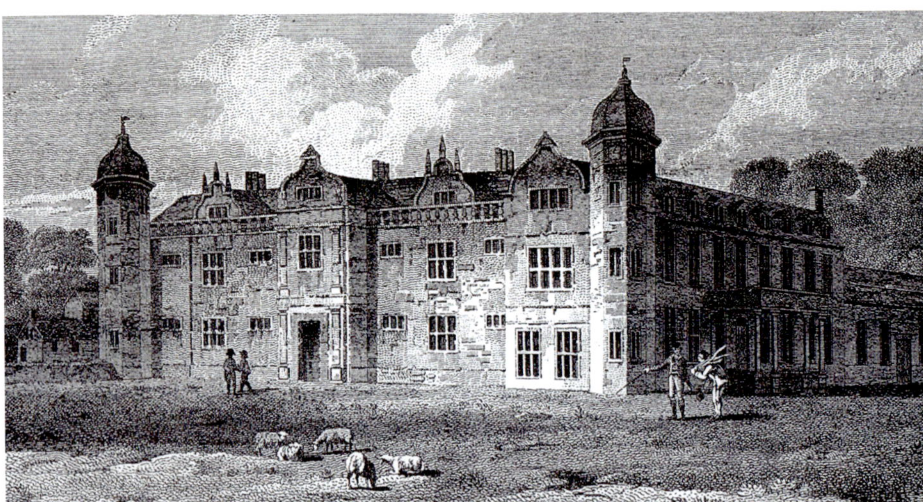

New House engraved by J. C. Smith after a drawing by T. Harris of 1702. (Private collection)

3. Easy Hill, Broad St., Birmingham, Warwickshire. 1795

The printer, flamboyant atheist and Lunar Society associate John Baskerville (1706–75) built a plain three-storey house here in 1747, four bays wide, two deep and otherwise quite plain, standing in a small park (in which Baskerville was buried, vertically, in a mausoleum topped by a windmill), approached by an avenue of trees, within the 7 acres of grounds, although the setting later became increasingly built up. Two drawings in Birmingham archives, showing the front and side elevations of the house, are in the hands of Joseph Pickford of Derby

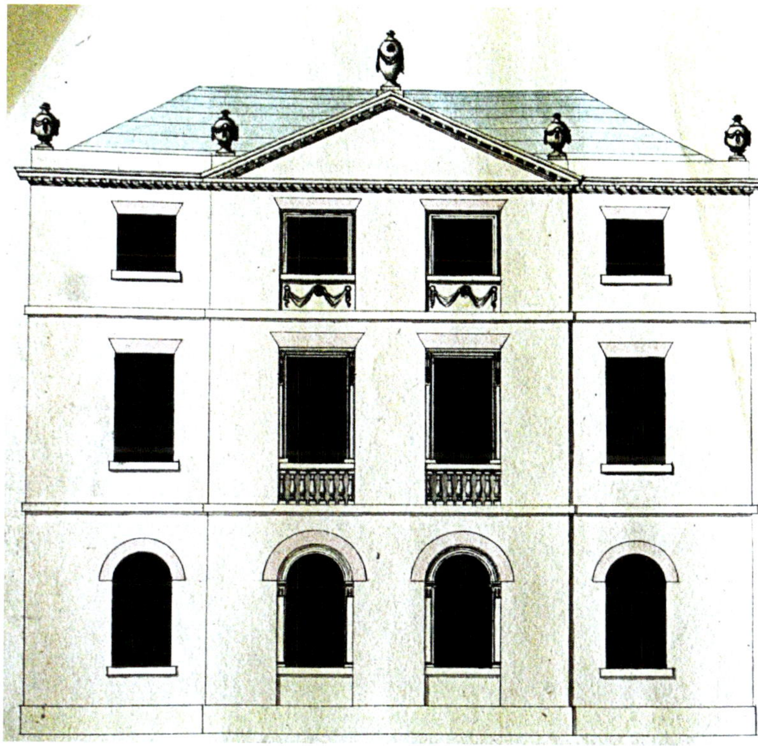

Easy Hill, drawing of the house as refronted, *c.* 1764. (Birmingham Archives)

(1734–82), architect of Sparkbrook House, nearby (q.v.), and clearly suggest that increasing property must have persuaded Baskerville to embellish and enlarge the building in Palladian style, presumably after Pickford first visited Baskerville's friend Matthew Boulton in Birmingham in 1760 and his death in 1782. On the death of Baskerville's widow in 1788 their daughter sold the house and estate, the particulars mentioning a stable, coach house, good garden, greenhouses, a grotto, garden house, and shady walks within its grounds, along with around 7 acres of pasture. It was bought by John Ryland (1726–1814), but the house was burnt out in the Church and King riot of July 1791, Ryland choosing to clear the remains in 1795. The site, sold by Samuel Ryland, was quickly built over and is now host to the former Birmingham Civic Centre, now called Baskerville House.

The house was burnt out in the Church and King riot of July 1791 and Ryland chose to clear the remains in 1795. The site, sold by Samuel Ryland, is now host to the former Birmingham Civic Centre, now called Baskerville House.

4. Birmingham Manor House, Warwickshire. 1815

By the third quarter of the twelfth century Peter de Birmingham had built a *castrum* on the western edge of the future city of Birmingham. Sir William de Birmingham was supposed to have been summoned as a baron in 1331, but this is widely doubted. His line ended with Thomas *c.* 1400, but the estate reverted to a collateral branch, of which Edward Birmingham was given in wardship to

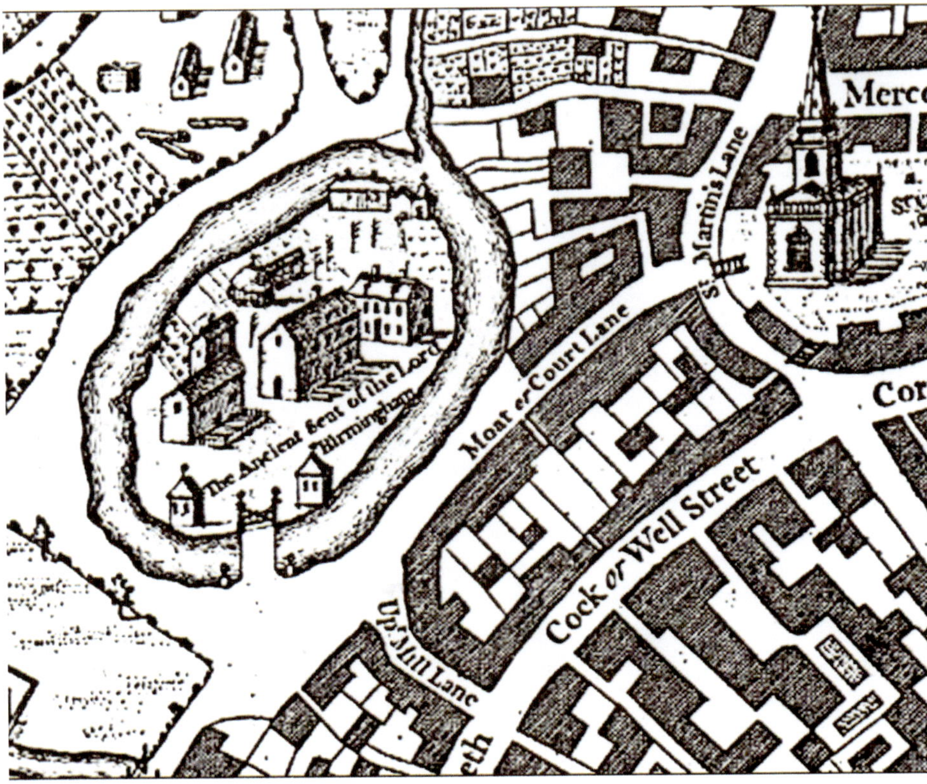

The Manor House and its moat as seen on William Westley's map of 1731. (M. Craven)

Edward, Lord Dudley, and who was deprived of the estate in 1540 by the son, John Dudley, afterwards Duke of Northumberland, after whose fall in 1553 it came in the hands of a family called Francis. The medieval house was said to have been long in ruins in 1527. Thomas Francis, a manufacturer, built a new house within the moat in 1732 according to Hutton, but the site was cleared and the moat filled in 1815–16.

5. Langley Hall, Walmley, Warwickshire. 1817

Langley Hall was originally a fortified moated manor house which Edmund de Beresford of Wishaw was given a licence to crenellate in 1327, the family having held it from the Earls of Warwick since the mid-thirteenth century. It passed via Edith Hore, who married Rowland Pudsey *c.* 1500, and the Pudsey family were there until Henry Pudsey died in 1677. Whilst his widow married carver and architect Sir William Wilson, one of her daughters, Anne, brought it to William Jesson of Four Oaks, who had Wilson rebuild the house and the nephew, Pudsey Jesson, sold to Andrew Hacket of Moxhull, mid-eighteenth century.

George Adderley Hackett inherited it in 1815, but he sold the estate to Sir Robert Peel in 1817, who demolished the house. Its moat and the substantial three-range brick stable block of *c.* 1685 attributed to Sir William Wilson survives, latterly derelict, until 1980 when it was sold and in 1987 converted into twelve residences with dormers facing the interior courtyard. It is Grade II listed. The Victorian Langley House was built on the site of the hall.

6. Willingsworth Hall, Sedgley, Staffordshire. *c.* 1836

The hall was built by the Parkes family, allegedly in 1510, and it was originally called Parkes Hall, a name which must have been current considerably earlier as there was a local yeoman family called Parkeshall in the parish in 1655. Some sources claim that it was brick, and 'large', but the date is really too early for brick to have been likely here, and an undated drawing shows the house to have been half-timbered with a timber-framed core. Richard Parkes was in possession in 1613, and under his son Thomas (d. 1660), a Parliamentary officer, it was captured and despoiled by the Royalists.

It passed in 1672 by marriage of Anne Parkes to Hon. William Ward, who enlarged it, hence in 1674 the house was assessed for tax on twenty-four hearths, one of the largest totals in Staffordshire. Their grandson John succeeded as 6th Lord Dudley and Ward (later 1st Viscount Dudley) and it was absorbed into the Dudley estate and tenanted. It finally was cleared to allow the expansion of the Willingsworth blast furnaces around 1836. The drawing of the house in the William Salt Library, Stafford, of a decade later may be unreliable, having been made from memory.

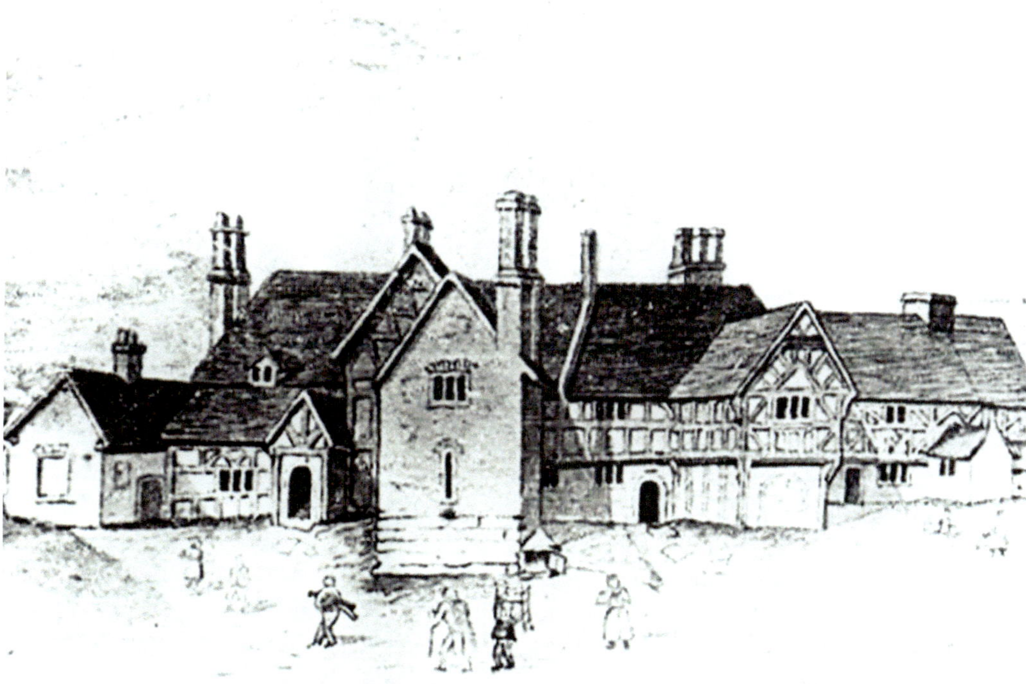

Willingsworth Hall, from a drawing of 1846 labelled 'Parkeshouse', showing the house in its later days. (William Salt Library)

7. Bordesley Hall, Birmingham, Warwickshire. 1840

The ancient manorial estate was in 1370 granted by Sir John Botetourt to Sir Hugh Segrave, whose widow brought it to Sir Thomas Blount. By 1563 it was in the hands of the Ardens, but on the death of Robert Arden in 1643, the estate was divided four ways amongst heiresses and was only reunited by purchase by Sir Charles Holte, 3rd Baronet, whose successors sold it to John Taylor in 1757, who was about to serve as High Sheriff of Warwickshire. He built a new house, finished in 1767, of two storeys. The entrance had a Venetian window over it with a balustrade above, flanked by a pair of canted bays rising, unusually, to an extra storey, the whole being flanked by lower, three-bay pavilions connected by links. He also created a 40-acre park with a lake, island, bridge and grotto, spending some £10,000. However, the hall was burned out during the Church and King riot in July 1791, and the younger John Taylor, having suffered, according to Hutton, a loss of £22,600, removed to Moseley Hall (q.v.). The ruins were still standing in 1818, when recorded by Sir Charles Pye, Baronet, and the site appears to have been cleared by or in 1840 for building.

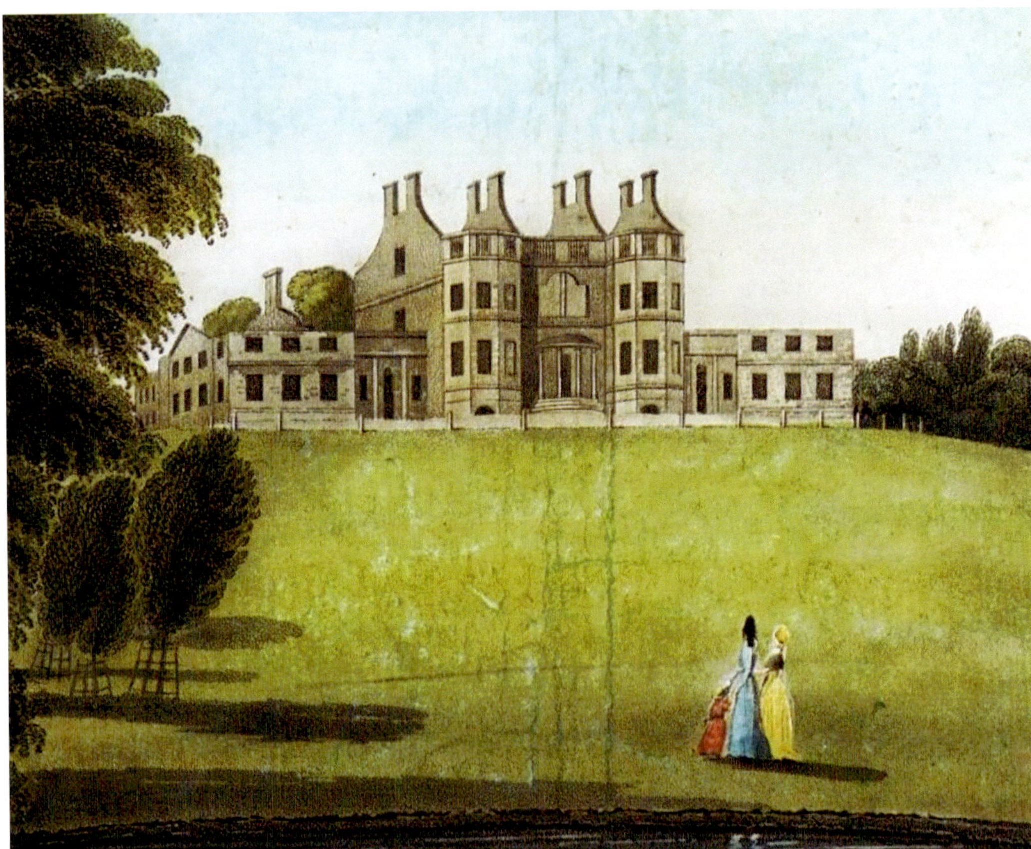

Colourised mezzotint of Bordesley Hall's gutted ruins from the park, by P. H. Whitton, 1791. (James Darwin)

8. Rushall Hall, Walsall, Staffordshire. 1845

The standing and buried remains of an important medieval fortified house lurk out of sight near the parish church hidden behind an anodyne row of interwar houses in Leigh Road. Late in the fourteenth century Geoffrey Ive of Henley-in-Arden, replaced an earlier hall of Sir Hugh de Boweles, who had been there from *c.* 1230 having inherited from the Rushalls. His heiress Eleanor married John Harpur in 1430, who built a fortified house within a moat, graced with a 21-foot tower, to which they added a late fifteenth-century gatehouse raised to three storeys in the early seventeenth century, access to which was via a circular stair in the north-east angle bearing the Harpur arms, which is the only substantial portion now remaining, albeit much mangled by the passage of time. The Harpurs' heiress married William Leigh of Shawell, Leicestershire, and his posterity rebuilt the house in the late sixteenth or early seventeenth century. During the Civil War, the Leighs were for Parliament but the house was captured by Prince Rupert in 1643 but regained by Parliament in 1644 under Col Lane and was promptly slighted. Nevertheless, the Leighs repaired the house itself and were resident owners until 1811 when the estate passed to the Mellish family. The gatehouse was demolished *c.* 1845 but recorded by J. C. Buckler in a watercolour. A nineteenth-century house which incorporates medieval remains occupies part of the site, but an archaeological excavation in 2011 uncovered the remains of a stone building of thirteenth- or fourteenth-century date. Its chapel was replaced by a surviving Victorian church.

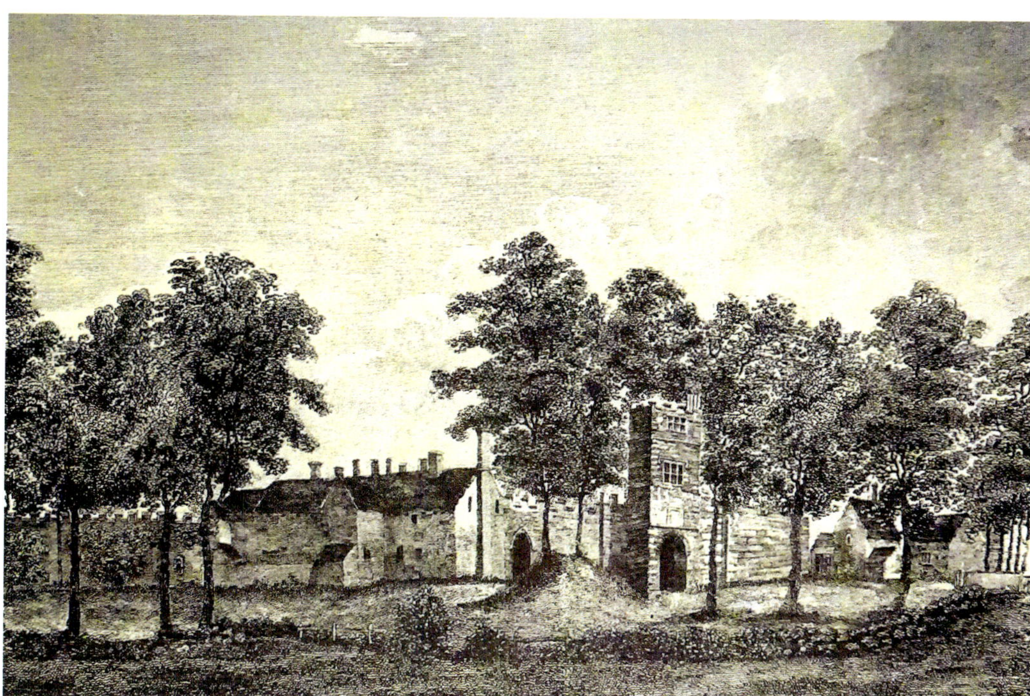

Rushall Hall, general view of 1801, Stebbing Shaw. (M. Craven)

9. Bingley House, Broad Street, Birmingham, Warwickshire. 1850

Bingley House was built by James Farmer, a Birmingham entrepreneur, in 1768 to replace an earlier house recorded in 1553 as Byngas Hall. It was a simpler version of Bordesley Hall and was possibly by the same hand, consisting of a pedimented entrance with a Venetian window over, flanked by a pair of deep canted bays all topped by a tallish parapet and given horizontal emphasis with a sill band. It was probably lower and broader than the engravings suggest. On either side were a pair of two-bay, two-storey, but lower, pavilions connected by links. Farmer's daughter and heiress Mary brought it in 1774 to her husband, Charles Lloyd (1748–1828), the Quaker banker, philanthropist, and anti-slavery campaigner, whose father founded what is now Lloyds Bank. The couple had fifteen children, the eldest being the poet Charles Lloyd (d. 1839). Their daughter Priscilla married the brother of the poet William Wordsworth. The last member of the family in residence there was Charles's brother James Lloyd (b. 1776), who in 1849 sold the estate for railway building, and the erection of a temporary exhibition hall, and was demolished the following year. The exhibition centre Bingley Hall was built to a design by the young J. A. Chatwin in the remaining grounds soon afterwards.

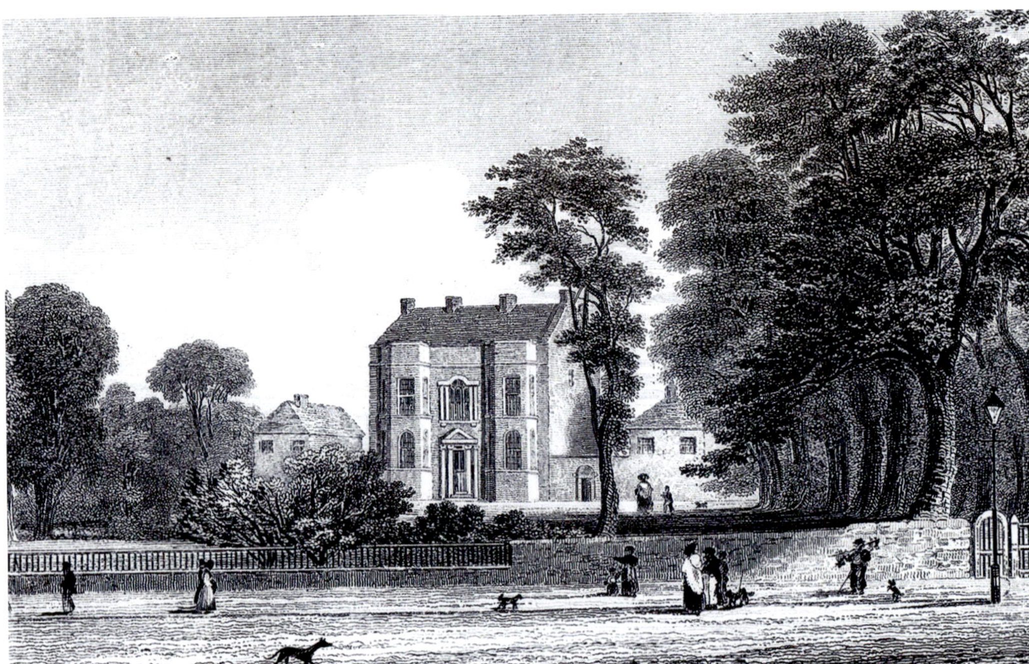

Bingley House, engraved in 1830 when still the home of James Lloyd. (James Darwin)

10. Smethwick Grove, Smethwick, Staffordshire. *c.* 1868

A late Georgian brick villa of two storeys, five bays, entrance front with a portico, and a hipped roof behind a parapet set in a well-wooded park of 59 acres with an artificial lake, built and laid out for the gunmaker Edward Walker, who died here

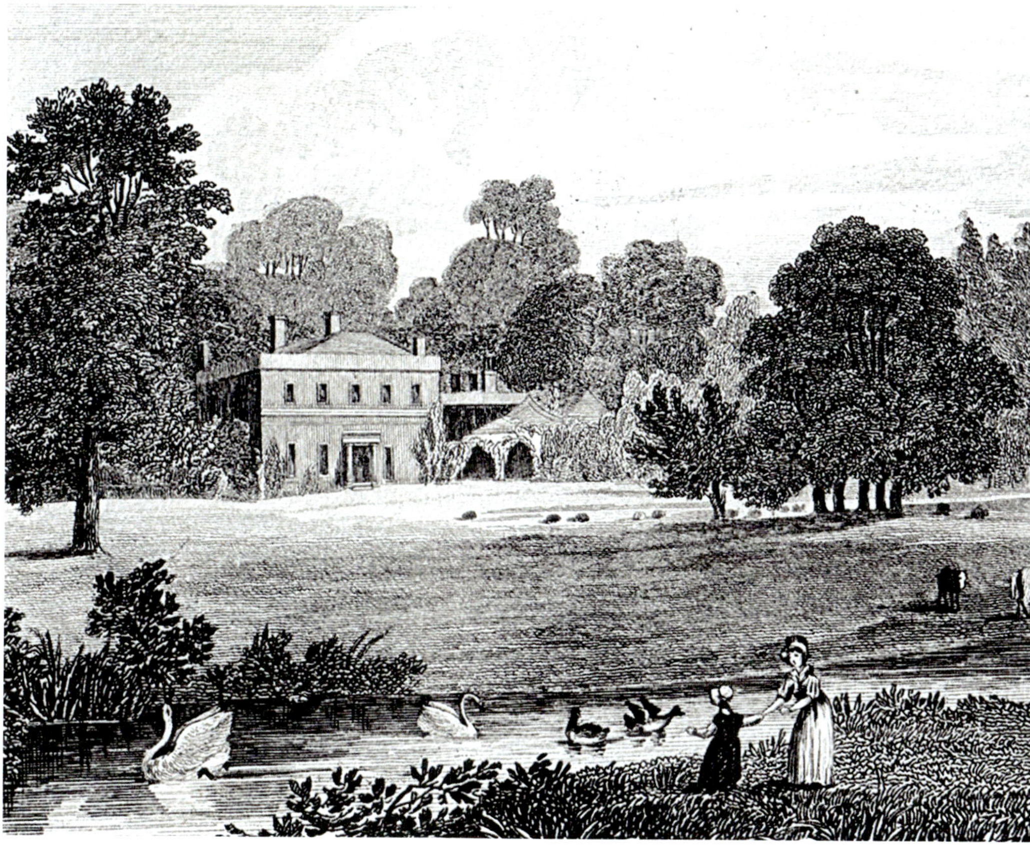

Smethwick Grove, from a drawing by Calvert engraved by T. Radcliffe, *c.* 1830. (James Darwin)

in 1798. Lunar Society member James Keir FRS (1735–1820) purchased the house from Walker's heirs, but was staying with friends when it caught fire in December 1807, although his papers and much else were saved. He was in residence at his death, when it passed to his daughter Amelia (1780–1857) and her Swiss banker husband John Lewis Moilliet. They let it to George Bacchus and went to live at Hamstead Hall, Handsworth (q.v.), after which it was let to Thomas Adkins, there in 1841, and George Selby, in the mid-nineteenth century. Thomas Gibson was its last occupier but by then the area was becoming increasingly industrialised and a factory was built within the grounds for George Selby, by which time it was unoccupied and was probably demolished for the construction of Guest Keen and Nettlefold's works.

11. Hockley Abbey, Hockley Heath, Warwickshire. *c.* 1870

A picturesque Gothic house with shaped gables of *c.* 1770, according to Charles Pye's *A Description of Modern Birmingham* (1818) it was built of iron furnace slag. It was built for Richard Ford, a thimble manufacturer and inventor, and came complete with an attached folly – a ruined abbey wall embellished with the spurious date of 1473 in pebbles. Ivy was deliberately trained over the structure

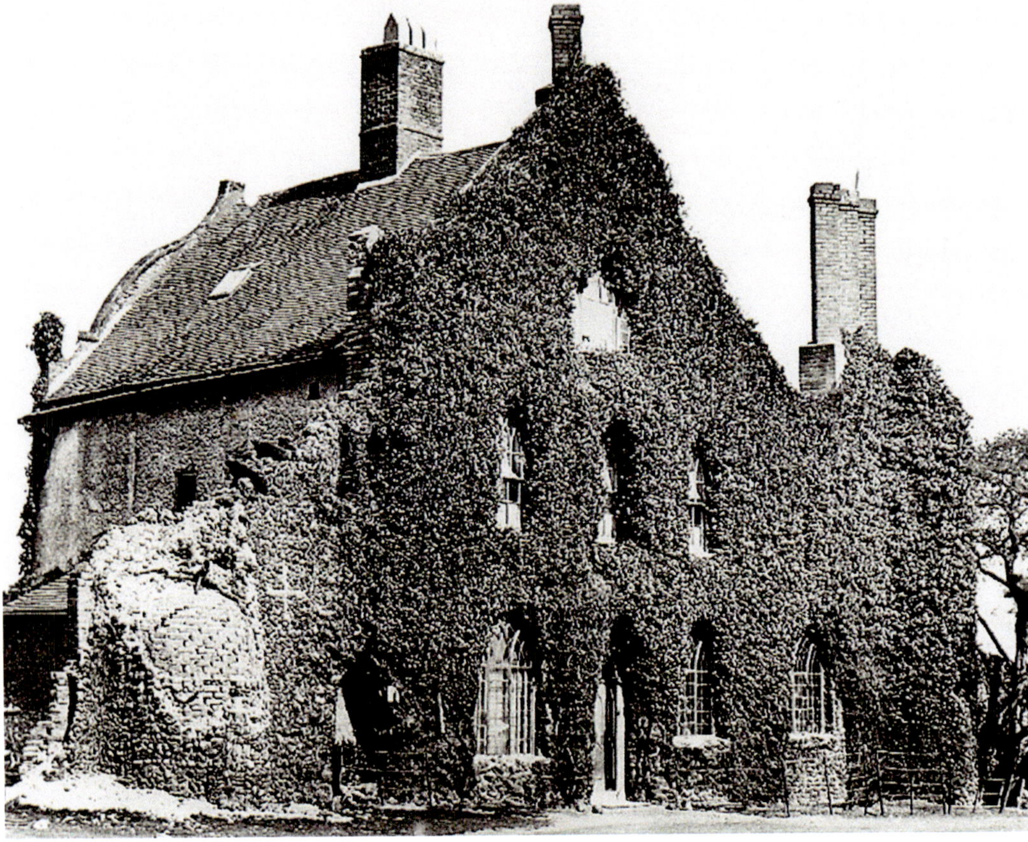

Hockley Abbey, from the south-west, photographed in the 1860s. (Private collection)

to increase its picturesque effect. A close examination of surviving photographs suggests, however, that the entrance elevation was in fact largely of rendered brick, whilst the carefully trained ivy may also have been planted to hide other areas of brickwork on the garden façade (shown here). This does not, however, diminish the house's undoubted eccentricity and interest. The slag was probably therefore mostly used as a decorative facing. The small estate of around 15 acres was let in 1818 to Hubert and Sophia Galton and then in the 1830s to James Hunt. In the mid-nineteenth century, Hockley Abbey was the home of the wire manufacturer G. F. Muntz, by which time its setting was becoming increasingly urbanised. Close to the house was an octagonal dovecote which was also partially faced in slag. Rabone's Hockley Abbey Works was built on or near its site in the 1870s. Birmingham Museums Trust own an atmospheric Victorian oil painting of the house in winter.

12. Sparkbrook House, Spark Hill, Warwickshire. 1871

John Taylor (1711–75) went into partnership with Charles Lloyd in 1765 to form the Birmingham Bank, an antecedent of Lloyds Bank. Taylor built

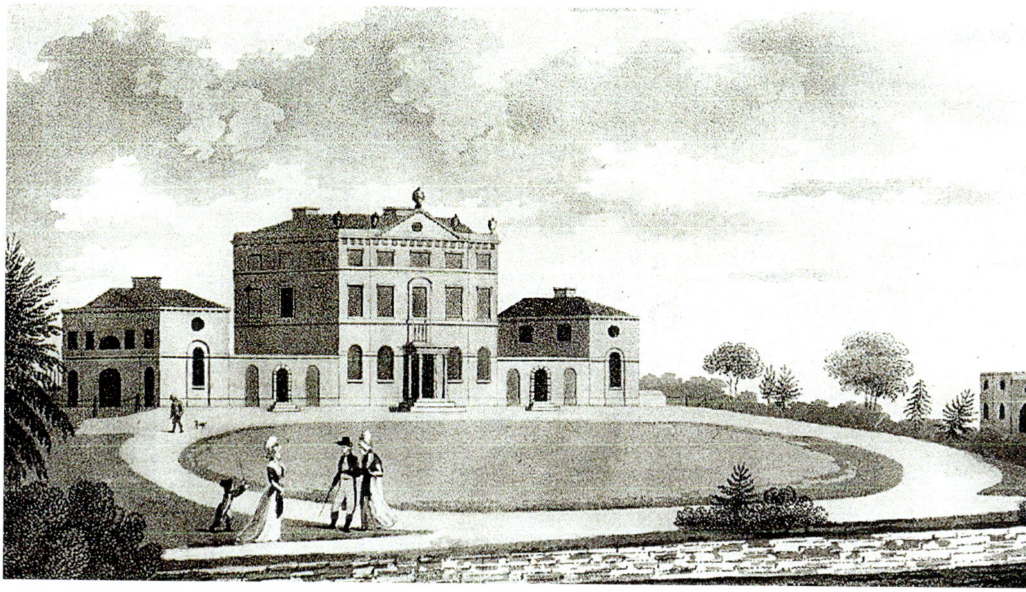

Sparkbrook House in 1791 after P. H. Whitton. (M. Craven)

Bordesley Park (q.v.), and the year after that, in 1768, purchased the manor and estate at Yardley. On his death in 1775, his younger son Charles inherited the Yardley estate, upon which he built the house, which had much in common with contemporary Sandon Hall, by Joseph Pickford of Derby, who records a visit to the area in 1776. It was of brick, two and a half storeys and five by three bays, the central three bays broke slightly forward under a pediment. There were three bay links and end pavilions. Below the house, nearer the road, was a curious Gothic stable block. In the 1780s, Charles Taylor moved to Moseley Hall, letting Sparkbrook House to a manufacturer called George Humphrey, who was living there when the famous Church and King riot of July 1791 broke out, the house being spared fire but was duly ransacked. As Moseley Hall actually was burned, Charles Taylor had to move back to Sparkbrook and his family remained there until his death in 1812. The house was thereafter let to the Wrights and finally to Samuel Thornley 1866–70 whilst Gilbertstone (q.v.) was being built, although the Taylors, from 1817 of Strensham Park, Worcestershire, continued to own the estate. It appears to have been demolished for redevelopment in 1871.

13. Larches (The), Sparkbrook, Warwickshire. *c.* 1871

Originally known as Fairhill, the house was built in 1780–81 for Lunar Society latecomer Revd Joseph Priestley FRS (1733–1804) but was burnt out in the 1791 riots, in which he lost everything, later retiring to the USA. His fellow Lunar Society member William Withering MD, FRS (1744–1799) bought the site and had the house completely rebuilt as The Larches, but died within months of its completion. This incorporated Priestley's house rebuilt, but a wider, five-bay range was added to the front, with entablatures over the windows, a separate

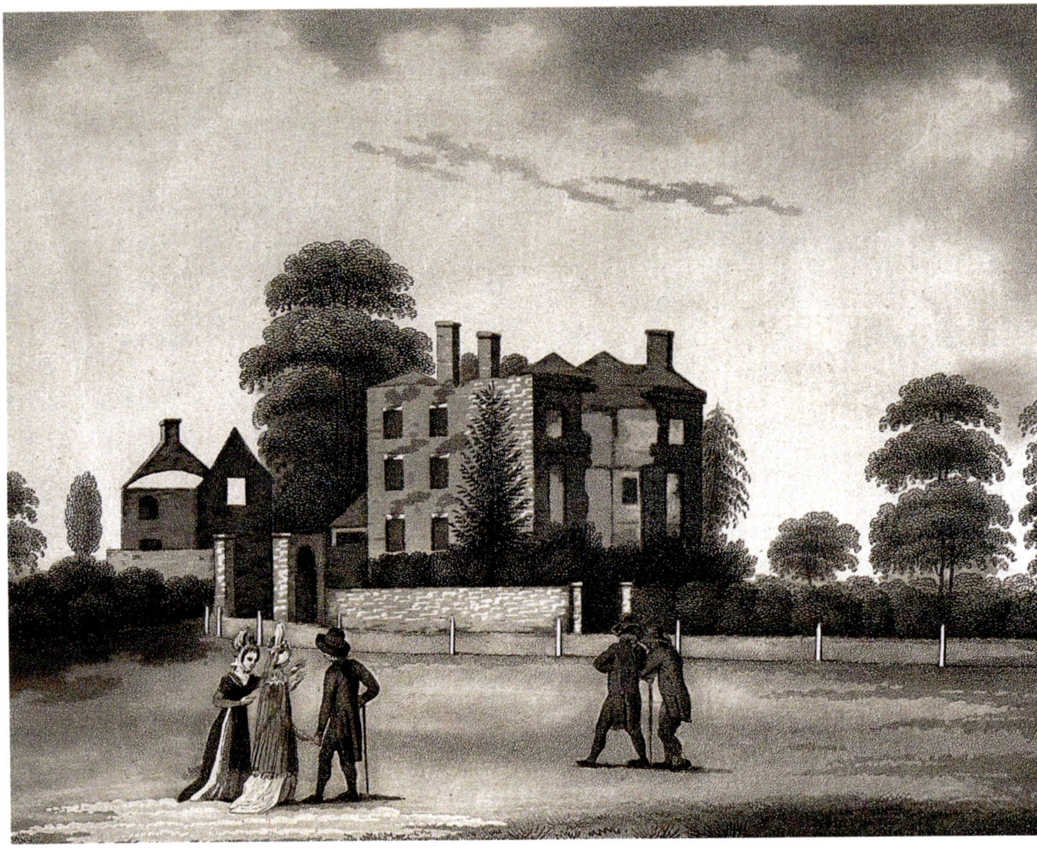

Fair Hill, as gutted in the riot, 1791, after P. H. Whitton. (Private collection)

hipped roof and a portico, later stuccoed. It had numerous outbuildings, one of which, the brewhouse, had previously been Priestley's laboratory. After Withering's death the house was sold to the banker and gunmaker Samuel Galton FRS and his wife Frances (née Darwin) and was the birthplace of Sir Francis Galton in 1822. Later it was the property of John Wilkes Unett, but the estate was for sale in 1856 with a sizeable portion marketed as building land. It later became the residence of the banker Thomas Attwood before he moved to The Grove, Harborne, but it was demolished in 1871 and its remaining parkland developed for housing.

14. Prospect Hill House, Handsworth, Staffordshire. 1871

Prospect Hill House was a two-storey stuccoed classical villa under a hipped roof, set on Soho Hill, with pavilions linked to the main block by single-storey links with pairs of *oculi* flanking a door. It was built in 1784 for Francis Eginton (1737–1805), eminent glass painter and engraver. The architect may have been Samuel Wyatt, cousin of his wife, Maria (d. 1811), whom he had married in 1776. Behind the house was a separate building in matching style which housed Eginton's glass works. The house was sold by Eginton's widow

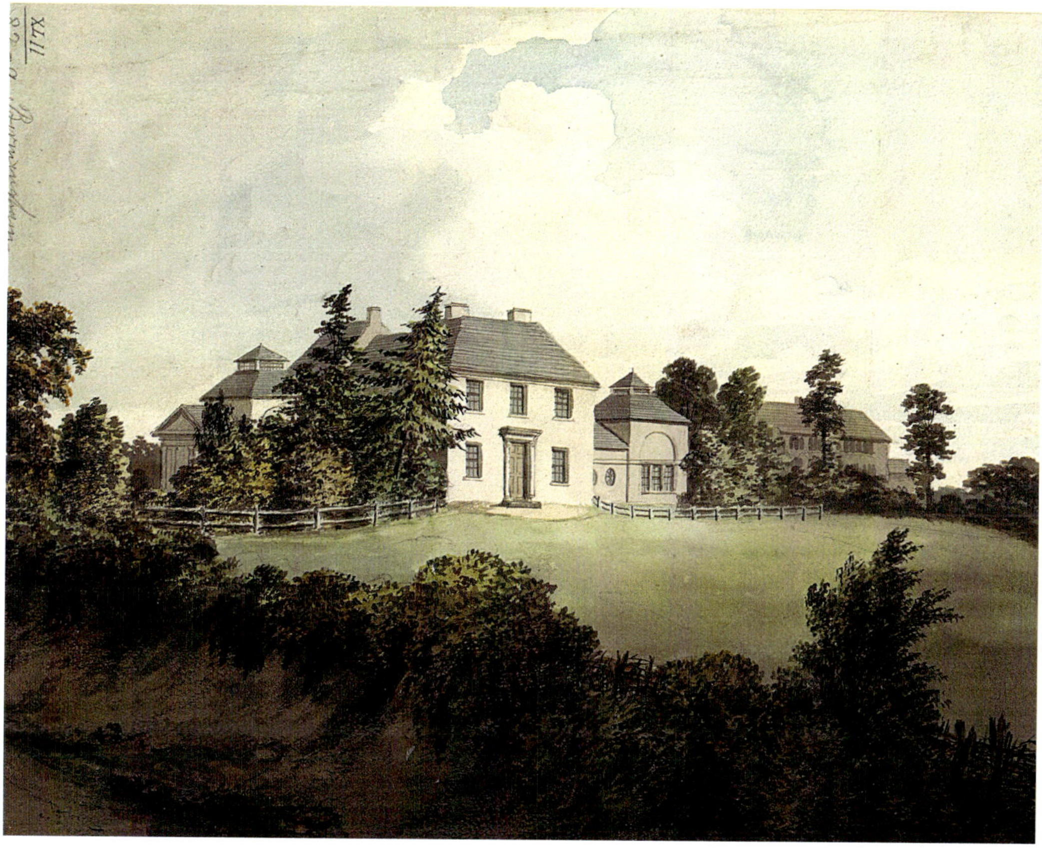

Prospect Hill House, 1786, artist unknown. (Wikimedia Commons)

Maria to Humphrey Evett in 1816 and then altered, subsequently passing via his granddaughter Mary to the Chapman family and William Floyd Chapman, who owned a carriage-making business, was in residence in 1855, by which date one of the wings and pavilions had been rebuilt and extended to form a drawing room and the other removed entirely. Less than two decades later, however, it had succumbed to redevelopment.

15. Coppice (The), Smethwick, Staffordshire. *c.* 1879

This villa had a relatively short life as a private house. It was probably built by the Reynolds family around 1814 and F. Calvert's engraving of 1830, when John Reynolds was living there, shows a two-storey, five-bay main block with a cornice so heavily dentilled as to appear like machicolations, behind which rose a hipped roof. It stood within 15 acres of 'ornamental pleasure grounds, laid out in Italian style'. The Reynolds later moved to Weston-on-Trent, Derbyshire, and let the house to William Wills, who sub-let to the liberal politician, second ever Mayor of Birmingham and industrialist Philip Henry Muntz, MP (1811–88) in the late 1840s. Muntz later moved to Edstone Hall, Warwickshire. Subsequently the house was owned by Thomas Gibson but was sold by him to the 4th Lord Calthorpe for

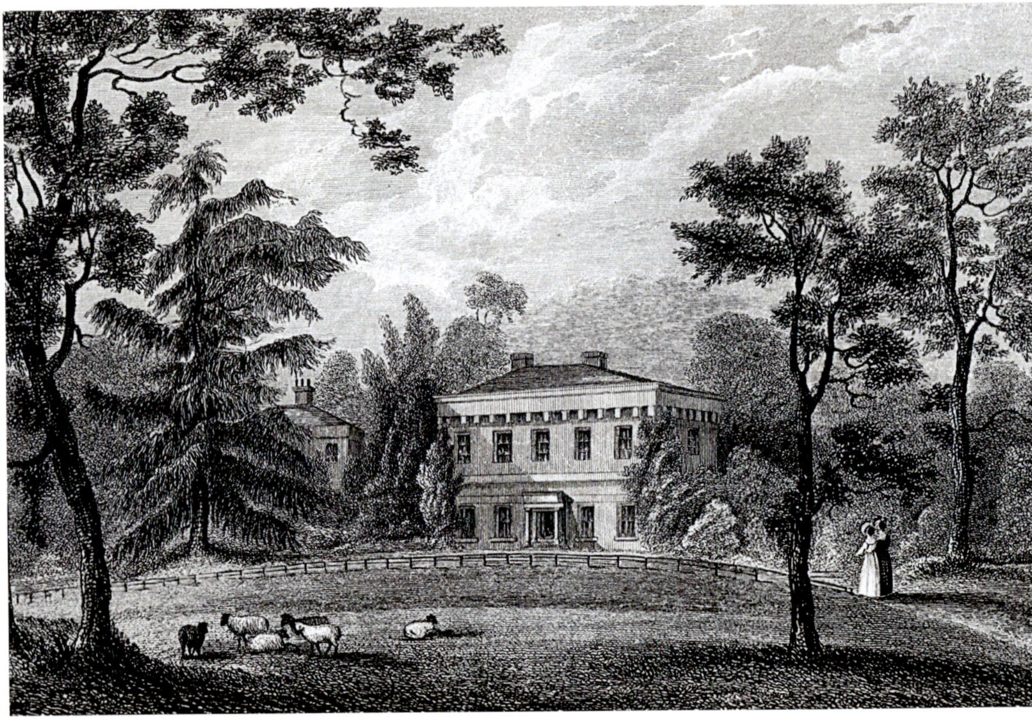

The Coppice, Smethwick, after F. Calvert, *c.* 1830. (James Darwin)

the creation of a girls' reformatory in November 1856. When this closed due to a typhoid outbreak, blamed on inadequate drainage, in September 1879, the house was demolished and the site redeveloped.

16. Wolverhampton Old Hall, Staffordshire. 1883

Richard Leveson (d. 1347) was granted the estate here by John de Pype, and it subsequently descended to wealthy wool merchant Thomas Leveson (d. 1563), whose house was noted by Leland. His heiress sold it to a cousin, John Leveson (d. 1575), also a Merchant of the Staple. The house is supposed to have been built in around 1570, a new brick prodigy house to replace a smaller timber-framed manor house. It was an impressive three-storey turreted building called the Great Hall, with projecting wings which was originally set within a large square moat, but the design, with family and state rooms on the upper floors, is closer to Worksop Manor in Nottinghamshire and may have been built a decade or so later. It descended to Sir Richard Leveson in 1661.Walter Leveson, having lost his son, sold it with its grounds, later called Ashmore Park, to the 1st Earl of Bradford in 1686/88, from whom it descended to Sir William Pulteney, Baronet, in 1801, from whom it came to the 1st Duke of Cleveland, its owner in 1832. None of these grandees wished to reside in the house, hence Joseph Turton took a long lease *c.* 1700 and removed the upper storey, making other alterations; it became known locally as Turton's Hall. Turton abandoned it as a dwelling *c.* 1735, although in 1767 part of the building was let to Messrs Jones & Taylor, Japanners, whilst the

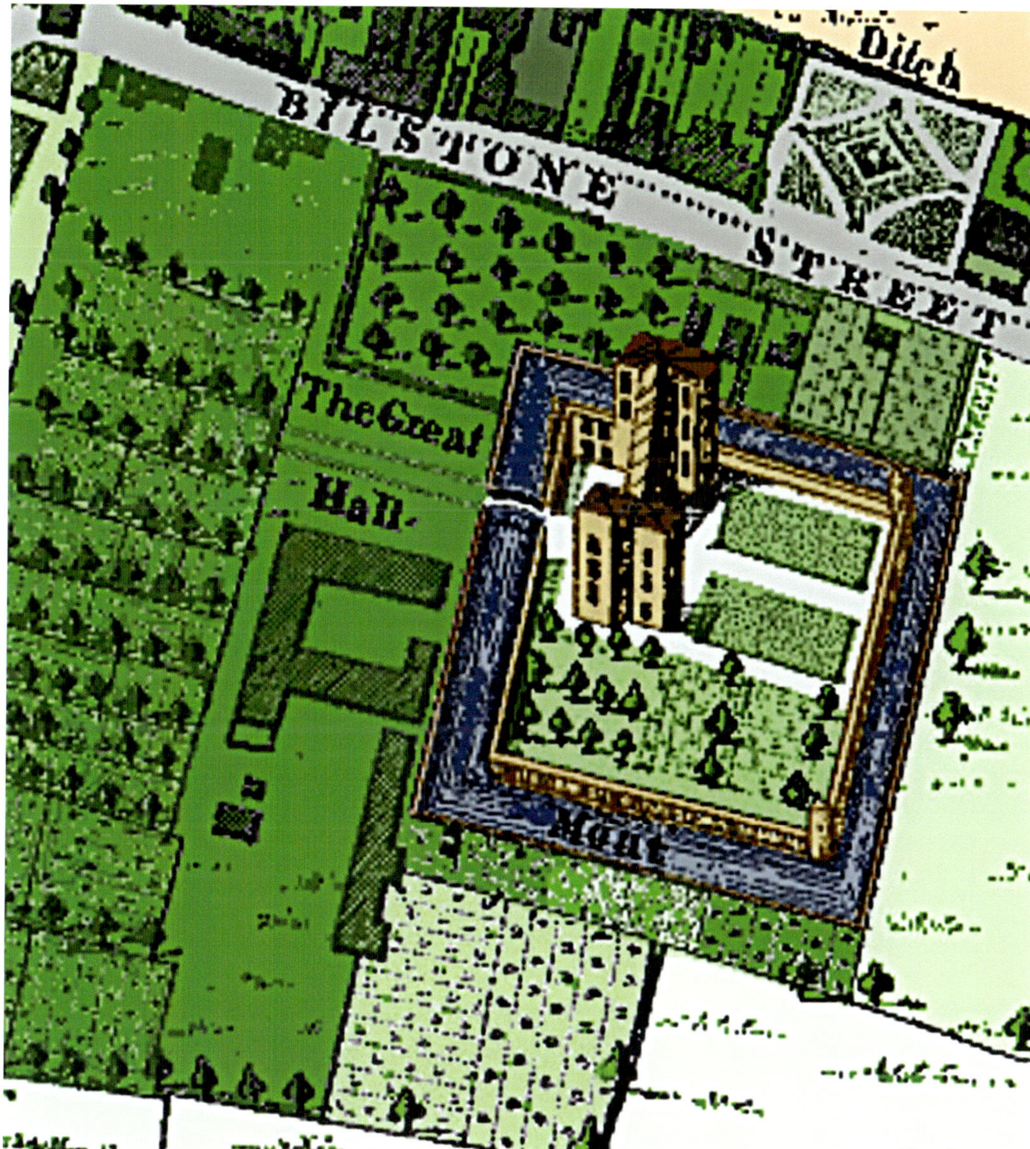

Wolverhampton Great Hall, from colourised Taylor's map, 1751. (M. Craven)

remainder remained the home of Dr. John Turton MD in 1801. By 1832 it was entirely given over to William & Obediah Ryton, who filled in the moat between then and 1842 when Walton & Co. held the lease. Excavations in 2002 found evidence of a wing dating from Turton's ownership, when parts of its grounds were also developed. Waltons moved out in 1883 when the building was subject of a sale, after which it was unceremoniously demolished, although part of its grounds survive as Ashmore Park.

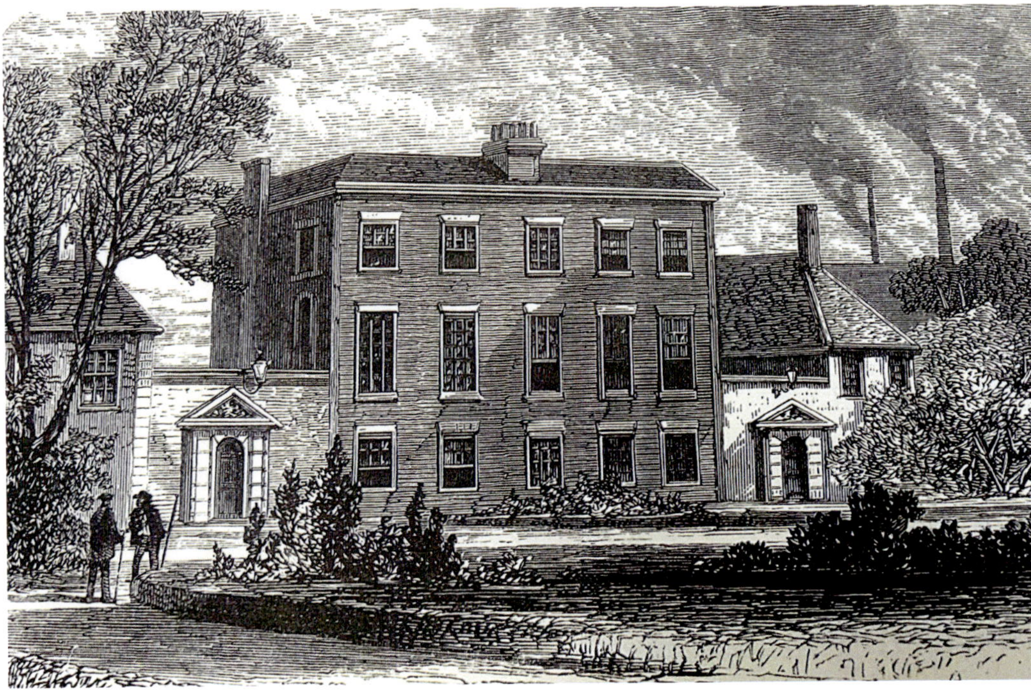

James Watt's Regent's Place (Harper's Hill House), as built, from Samuel Smiles, 1862. (M. Craven)

17. Harpers Hill House, Hockley, Warwickshire. 1885

The name only first came to record in 1772, shortly before the house was built in 1775 in brick on land leased from the Colmore estate. The client was new Lunar Society recruit James Watt FRS (1736–1819), who called it Regent's Place and lived there with his wife until 1790 when he moved to Heathfield at Handsworth (q.v.). It was a large three-storey house of brick with stone dressings, five bays wide, very plain under a hipped roof. There were two-storey linked pavilions each with tall hipped roofs and taller chimneys, each link having a rusticated and pedimented entrance. The house, subsequently Harper's Hill House, was divided into two dwellings after the Watts left and so remained until the industrial expansion of the jewellery quarter of Birmingham, on the edge of which it lay, forced its removal in 1885. Its surroundings had become heavily industrialised by the mid-nineteenth century and upon demolition it was replaced by workshops. The foundations of the house were uncovered during an archaeological excavation in 2021.

18. Summerfield House, Dudley Road, Birmingham, Warwickshire. *c.* 1894

This three-storey, three-by-four-bay Neo-Grec brick house had a Soanian *antae* at the angles, top parapet and a low pediment bookended by acroteria, built in 1828 for Robert Lucas Chance (1782–1865), whose firm, Chance Brothers, were glass makers who supplied much of the glass for the 1851 Great Exhibition, having

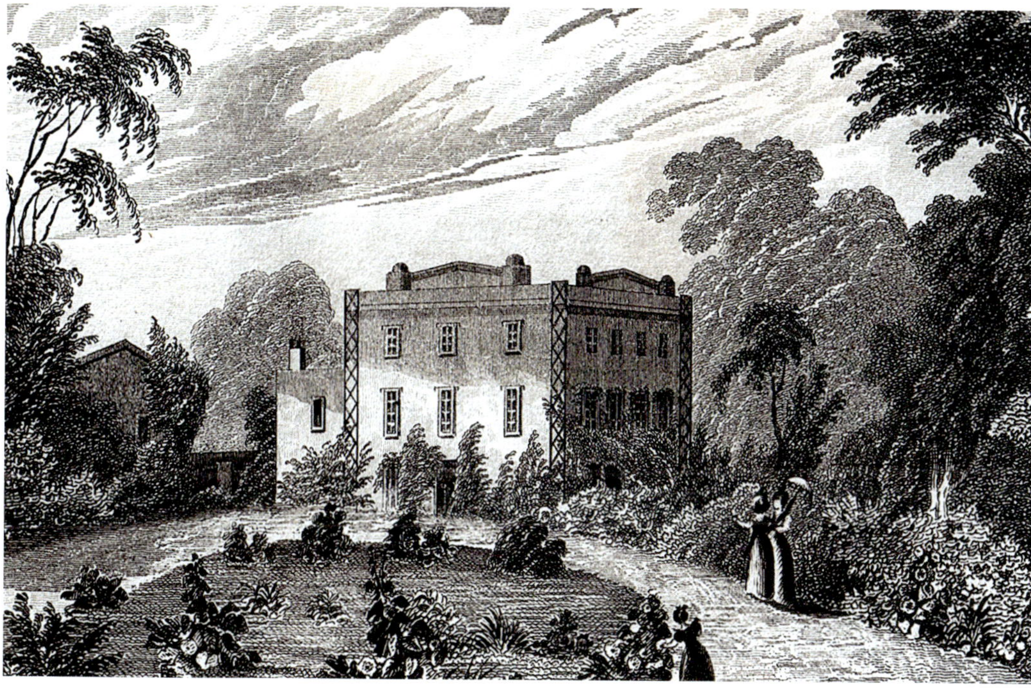

Summerfield House, *c.* 1830, after F. Calvert. (Private collection)

previously worked with Paxton on the construction of the now destroyed Great Stove at Chatsworth. Chance's widow Louisa remained at the house until her death in 1873 but by then her son had moved to Sussex and her grandson acquired an estate at Great Alne and the house was let. The 1889 OS map shows that at that time much of the house's setting had been developed for housing, but the house still stood in sizeable, wooded pleasure grounds approached via a lodge. Yet part of the estate had been sold to Birmingham Corporation in 1876 by Robert Lucas Chance II (1821–97) to form a small public park to which further parts of the former park including the house were added in 1890, the house being removed three years later, a rather elegant brick bandstand being constructed on its site.

19. Red Hill House, Washwood Heath, Warwickshire. *c.* 1896

The historian William Hutton (1823–15) bought some land on Bennett's Hill in 1769 and building began at once, Hutton observing with surprise that the workman cutting the first turf was 'engaged in prayer' before doing so. Red Hill House, as Hutton called his new home, is attributable to Joseph Pickford of Derby. It was completed and occupied before 1769 ended, the wings being added the following year, and the grounds landscaped in 1771. Hutton himself had moved to Birmingham and opened a paper warehouse in 1756. An engraving published in the *Gentleman's Magazine* in 1815 from a drawing by Parkes shows that it was tall and narrow, like Priestley's Fair Hill (cf. The Larches, qv) being of three storeys with attics, but three bays wide, under a pediment, all breaking

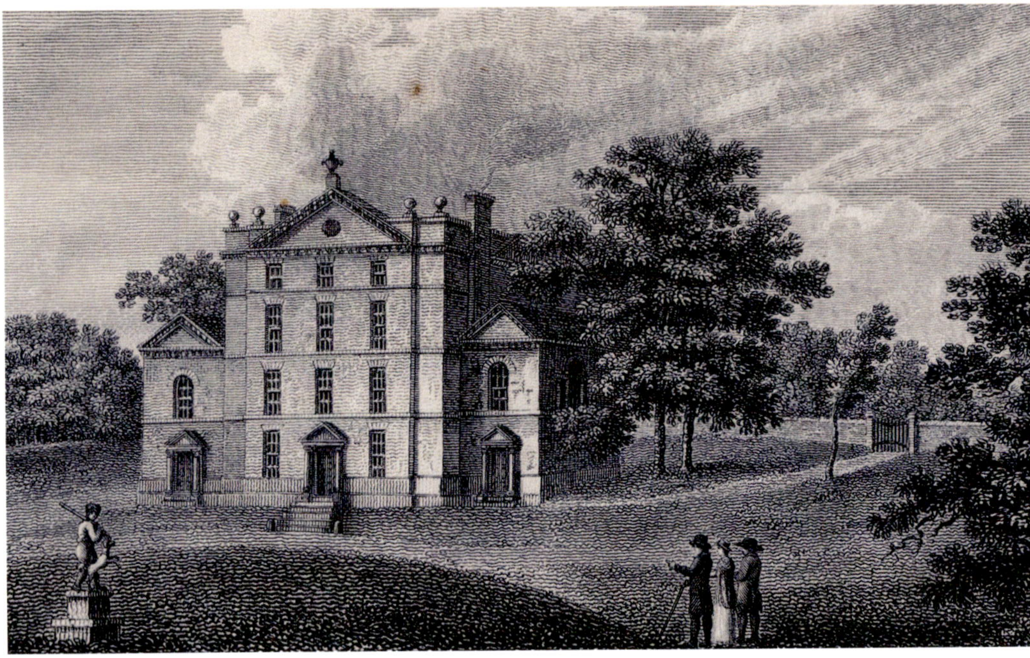

Red Hill House, as built, depicted in the *Gentleman's Magazine*, 1815. (James Darwin)

slightly forward. Pedimented single-bay, two-storey pavilions were attached either side, according to Hutton's autobiography, in 1770, with Venetian windowed returns. This arrangement is confirmed by his pre-fire full-length portrait, which shows the house in this guise (but looking distinctly less tall). Being an irascible Dissenter and a radical to boot, it will occasion no surprise to learn that the house was torched on 15 July 1791 during the Church and King riot at Birmingham, Whitton's mezzotint of 1792 showing it derelict and with both wings removed, which must have been done within weeks of the outbreak. It was rebuilt in the 1790s in a weird form of Adam-esque, but succumbed to the total clearance of the site in 1896. Bennett's Hill House (q.v.) was later built in the grounds for Hutton's son.

20. Allesley Hall, Allesley, Warwickshire. 1907

Allesley's castle belonged Henry de Hastings in the thirteenth century and he emparked the estate, which passed to the Earls of Warwick in the century following. In 1639 it was sold to Sir William Compton. His heir Richard sold in 1660 to Thomas Flint MP (d. 1670), whose widow sold to Henry Neale MP in 1692 with a house, but he set about building a new seat on the ridge overlooking the village: two and a half storeys, nine by five bays, both fronts pedimented, under a hipped roof in brick with busy quoins. In 1805 the house was inherited by Revd Edward Vansittart and tenanted by the 2nd Earl of Clonmell, then by the banker James Beck, who improved the gardens, but from 1848 until 1887 it was Allesley Park College. From 1887 to his death in 1897 it was purchased and lived in by Lt Col Francis Newdegate. It was then acquired by Charles and Edgar Turrall, cycle

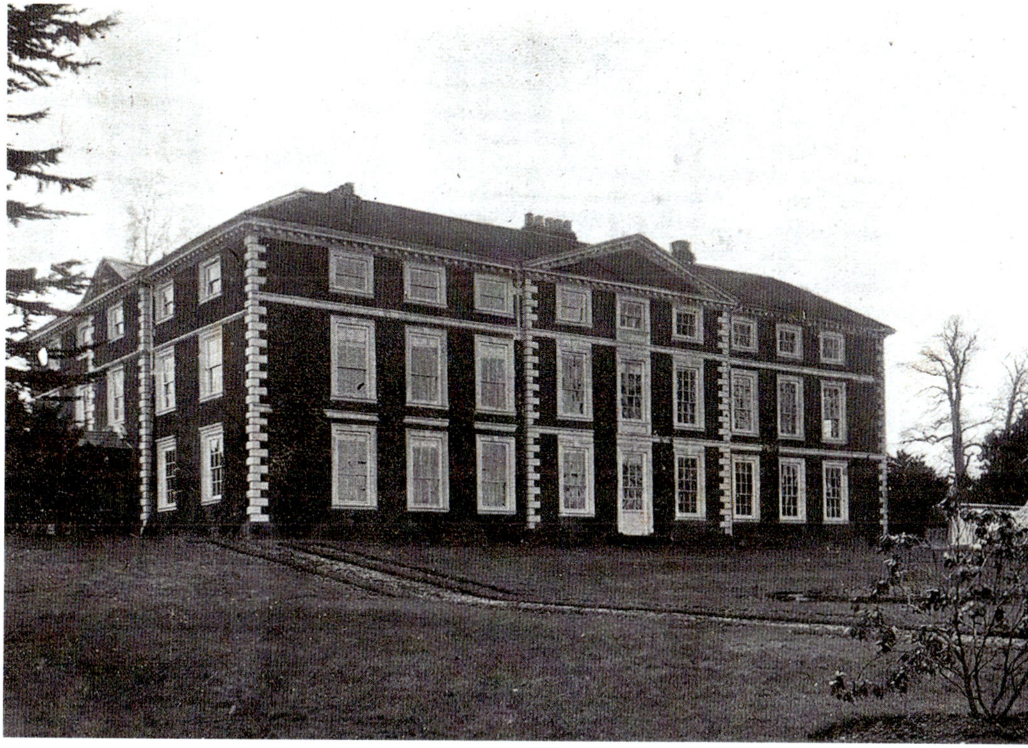

Allesley Hall, from the south-west, c. 1900, from a postcard. (James Darwin)

manufacturers, who reduced it and then sold it in 1906 to William Iliffe, whose son Edward was created 1st Lord Iliffe. He demolished the hall in 1907, replacing it with the present Arts and Crafts house designed by Harry Quick, completed in 1910 and currently a care home. The stable block and Beck's walled gardens survive.

21. Fulford Hall, Spark Hill, Warwickshire. *c.* 1897

A fifteenth-century timber-framed manor house with a jettied parlour cross wing of late sixteenth-century date, which was built on land belonging to Maxstoke Priory and taking its name from the medieval donor, Roger de Fulford, living 1275. It was acquired in 1547 by the Greswoldes of Greet, near Acocks Green, who added the cross wing, but later resided in Solihull, letting the old house as a farm, by the eighteenth century called Grove Farm, when it was the home of a Greswolde kinsman. The family became extinct with the death of John Greswolde of Solihull in 1760 and thereafter the estate descended from Henry Greswolde Lewis to the Wigley family and ultimately to the Greswolde-Williamses. The estate was slowly eaten away from the late 1840s for housing but the bulk of the estate, including the house, by then farmed by the Izod family, was sold in 1896 to the Freehold Land Society, who demolished the old house the following year and built terraced houses on the site, Grove Road marking its approximate location.

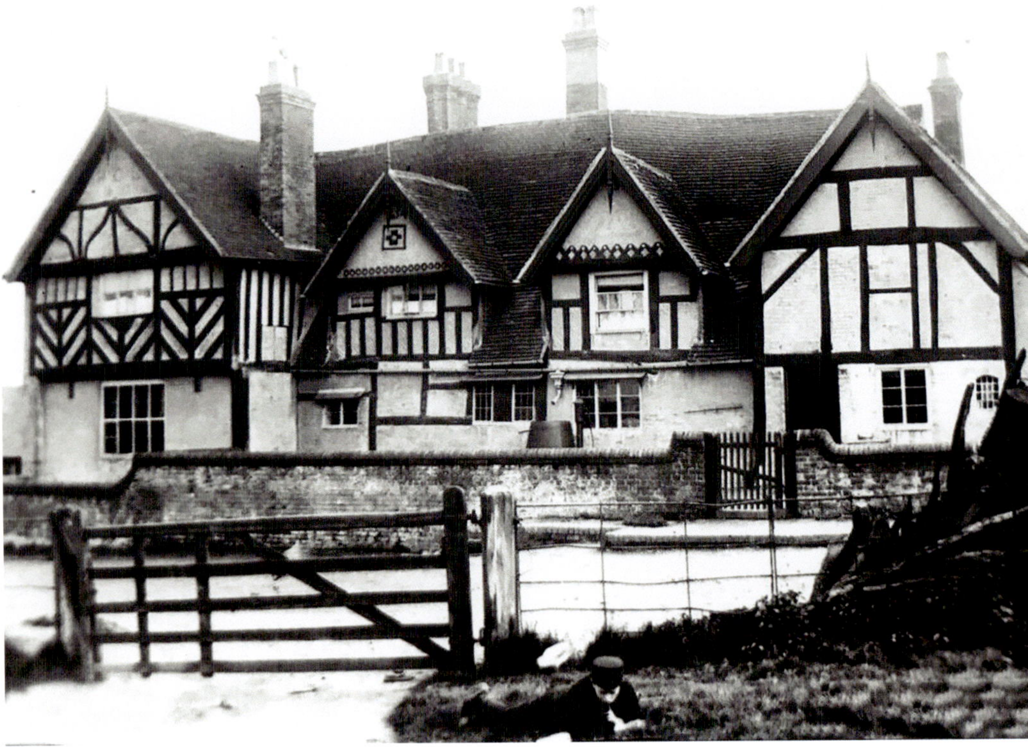

Fulford Hall, as Grove Farm, photographed in 1897 prior to demolition. (James Darwin)

22. Brown's Green House, Handsworth Wood, Staffordshire. 1898

Roger Brown held some land here in 1538 paying for it 2*s* 10*d* rent and hence bestowing his name upon it. The house appears to have been built in the last years of the eighteenth century by opulent barrister Nathaniel Gooding Clarke (1755–1833), also of Derby, who was in possession in 1801. He extended the original two-and-a-half-storey house in 1820 with a two-storey range to the east, removed the balusters from the parapet, added cast-iron sliding jalousies and rendered the lot in Roman cement. The architect for the alterations was almost certainly Richard Leaper of Derby, who had designed his villa there at about the same time. A Grade II listed and picturesque *cottage ornée* lodge, originally thatched, much in Leaper's style, remains but the icehouse succumbed in the 1950s. Clarke's elder son, Anthony, sold it in 1844 to the glass manufacturer Sir James Timmins Chance, 1st Baronet (1814–1902), but he sold in 1856, having taken a short lease on Four Oaks (q.v.). By 1870 it was used as a boarding school hall but ownership of the institution passed *c.* 1879 to the Lowe family, who

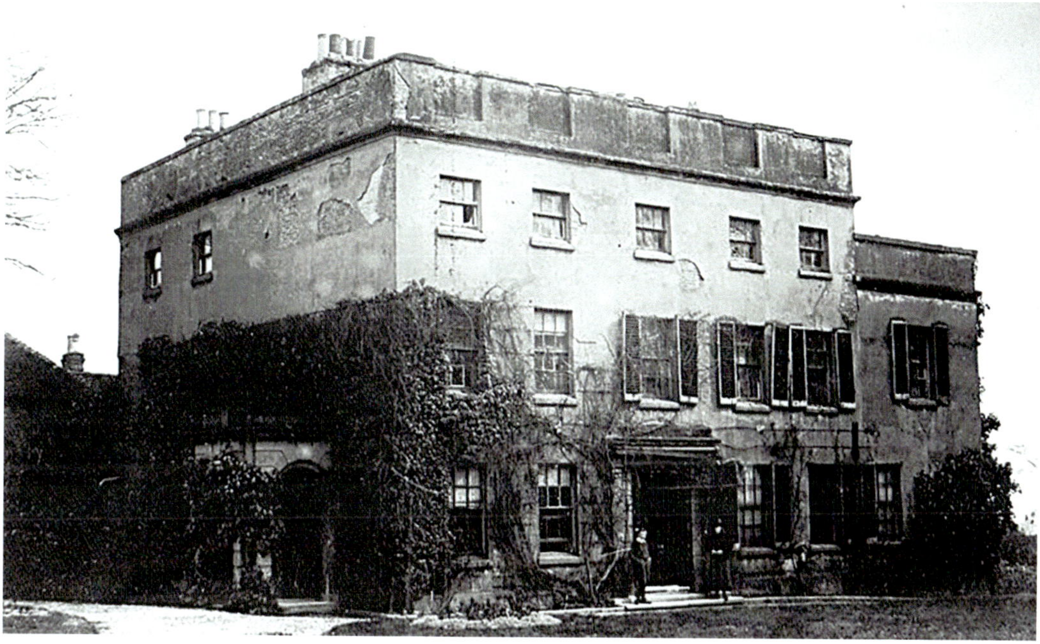

Brown's Green House as Hamstead Hill School, *c.* 1889. (Private collection)

changed its name to Hampstead Hill School. It was demolished for housing developments in 1898.

23. Four Oaks Hall, Sutton Coldfield, Warwickshire. 1899

Built by the 3rd Lord Folliott of Ballyshannon in 1696–97 on a new site, replacing an earlier seat of the Pudseys, whose co-heiress he had married, and designed by Folliott's kinsman William Wilson. The house was of two storeys with shaped gables to the cross wings. The Folliotts sold in 1744 to the rakish Irish aristocrat Simon Luttrell MP, later 1st Earl of Carhampton, who altered the house in the Palladian style, enclosing the 48-acre park, adding raised angle pavilions and a giant pedimented attached portico, possibly the work of William Hiorn. From 1766, however, the house was let and the estate mortgaged whilst the Earl retired to his County Dublin estate at Luttrellstown. The estate was sold in 1778 to Revd Thomas Gresley of Drakelow, Derbyshire, and it may be for him that the interior was altered, with a new principal stair with a delicate iron balustrade, the services and stables also being rebuilt. When Gresley died at Bath in 1785 it was leased to Sir Hugh Bateman (later 1st Baronet) of Derby, but in 1792 it was sold to Edmund Cradock Hartopp of Merevale and Scraptoft, Leicestershire. The park was extended in 1827. Whilst part of the park had been sold in 1868 for a short-lived racecourse, in 1880 Sir John Cradock-Hartopp, 4th Baronet, sold the rest for the development of 'desirable villas' (some of which are themselves listed buildings) and a railway station was built close to the house in 1884. The house finally succumbed to the contractor's ball in 1899.

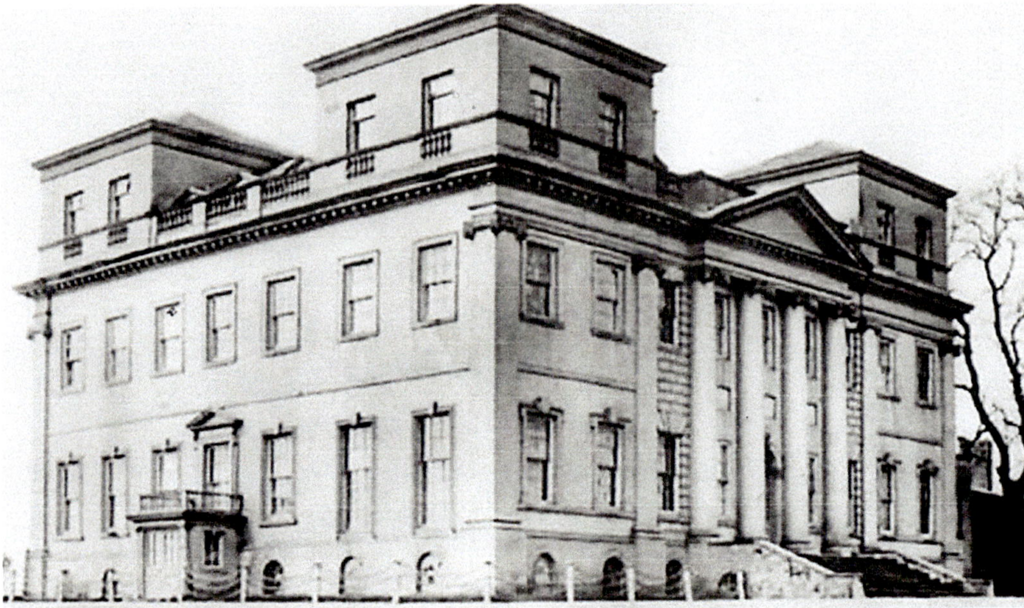

The rebuilt Four Oaks, photographed in the 1890s. (James Darwin)

24. Monument House, Edgbaston, Warwickshire. 1899

Originally called Rotton Park Lodge, its estate was granted by Queen Mary to Thomas Marrow in 1553 but sold by Sir Edward Marrow to Humphry Perrott *c*. 1630. The estate was inherited by John Perrott in 1737 and the house probably rebuilt by him. A fine painting of the family gathered outside their restrained classical brick mansion survives. He also built the now Grade II* listed viewing tower known as Perrott's Folly in 1758. John Perrott left the estate to his daughter Catherine, Mrs Walter Noel, on his death in 1776 but they lived at Belbroughton and the house was let. In 1825 part of the estate was sold for building Edgbaston reservoir. The house was later Gothicised and an early to mid-nineteenth-century wing of an eletic neo-Tudor design with both crenellations and gables was added and its name was changed to Monument House. Joseph Gillott purchased what remained of the estate in the late 1850 and developed it for housing. Maps suggest that the later wing then became a separate house. Many of the large first generation houses which were constructed in its grounds have also now gone, including Rotton Lodge, the neo-Tudor childhood home of Sir Bernard Docker, demolished in 1936 well before his later notoriety.

25. Thornhill House, Handsworth, Staffordshire. 1900

A three-storey red-brick classical house with a hipped roof, the house sat in extensive grounds behind a high brick wall. It was built in the later 1790s by John Scales, who worked at the Soho Manufactory, but was soon afterwards purchased by Matthew Boulton as the intended home of his daughter Anne and her prospective husband, Dr John Carmichael, but by 1804 the marriage

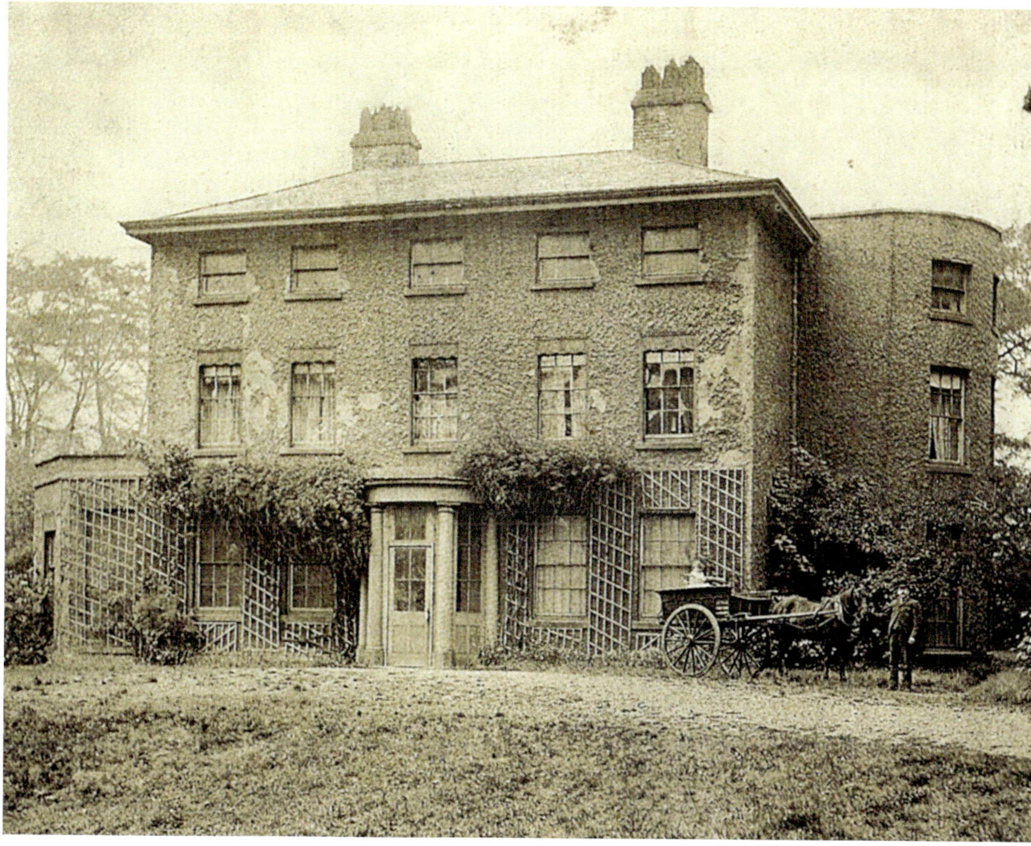

Thornhill House, Edgbaston, *c.* 1890. (Private collection)

was off. Boulton's letters suggest that he remodelled the interior of the house and undertook other improvements for his daughter. These alterations are likely to have included the canted bays and fine semicircular porch as they are shown on plans of 1820. The house was then let to James Watt Jr, who added a kitchen garden, George Bullock being commissioned to furnish and wallpaper the house. Anne Boulton nevertheless lived there from 1818 until her death in 1829, carrying out further alterations and improvements including work commissioned in 1823 from Rickman & Hutchinson. Later occupants included James Mason, a merchant, and Edward Chance. The house was demolished in 1900.

26. Sycamore Hill House, Handsworth, Staffordshire. *c.* 1900s

Engineer William Murdock (1754–1839) had built for himself a two-storey stuccoed villa with a stone Tuscan portico and hipped roof near the Soho works of his long-term employer, Matthew Boulton, in 1817, which he called Fair Hill, although the proximity of The Larches (q.v.), then also called Fair Hill, led to the renaming of both. There was a small park, pleasure grounds and the estate included a modest farm, Sycamore Farm, which took its name from the toponym.

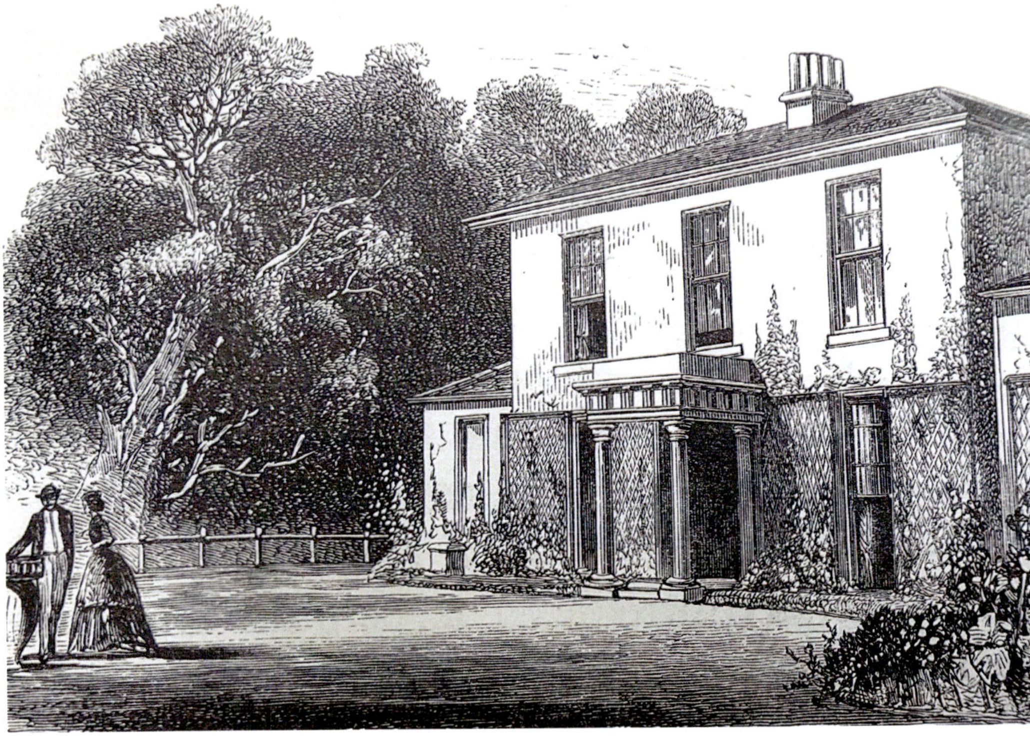

Sycamore Hill House, from Samuel Smiles, 1884. (M. Craven)

The house included a considerable number of those improvements in 'domestic economy' so beloved of Lunar Society improvers, including – naturally – gas lighting, hot water, WCs, a doorbell worked by compressed air and heating and ventilation systems derived from John Whitehurst's system as improved by Boulton and William Strutt. On Murdock's death the house was let, but soon fell into decline, for the opening of Handsworth railway station in 1854 rendered the land highly desirable for the building of genteel villas, and the estate was accordingly sold. By 1900 the building was in use solely as a store for building materials and was demolished soon afterwards.

27. Bournbrook Hall, Bournville, Worcestershire. *c.* 1907

Bournbrook was apparently built in the later eighteenth century for the Izons, who sold it *c.* 1827. It then became the home of Richard Stock, a glass and lead merchant, who altered the exterior. The contents of the house together with farm machinery were sold at auction in 1866. The estate was then sold or leased by his widow Sarah's executors *c.* 1866 to William Martin. The house boasted a pedimented five-bay principal façade with pilasters at the angles. Its ground floor was rebuilt to project out from the façade by Richard Stock *c.* 1830, and was lit by large tripartite windows. The house sat at the crest of a steep bank in well wooded grounds. The estate was purchased by the Cadburys in 1893 and the bulk of the grounds are now part of Bournville Park, a grandiose Tudor vernacular

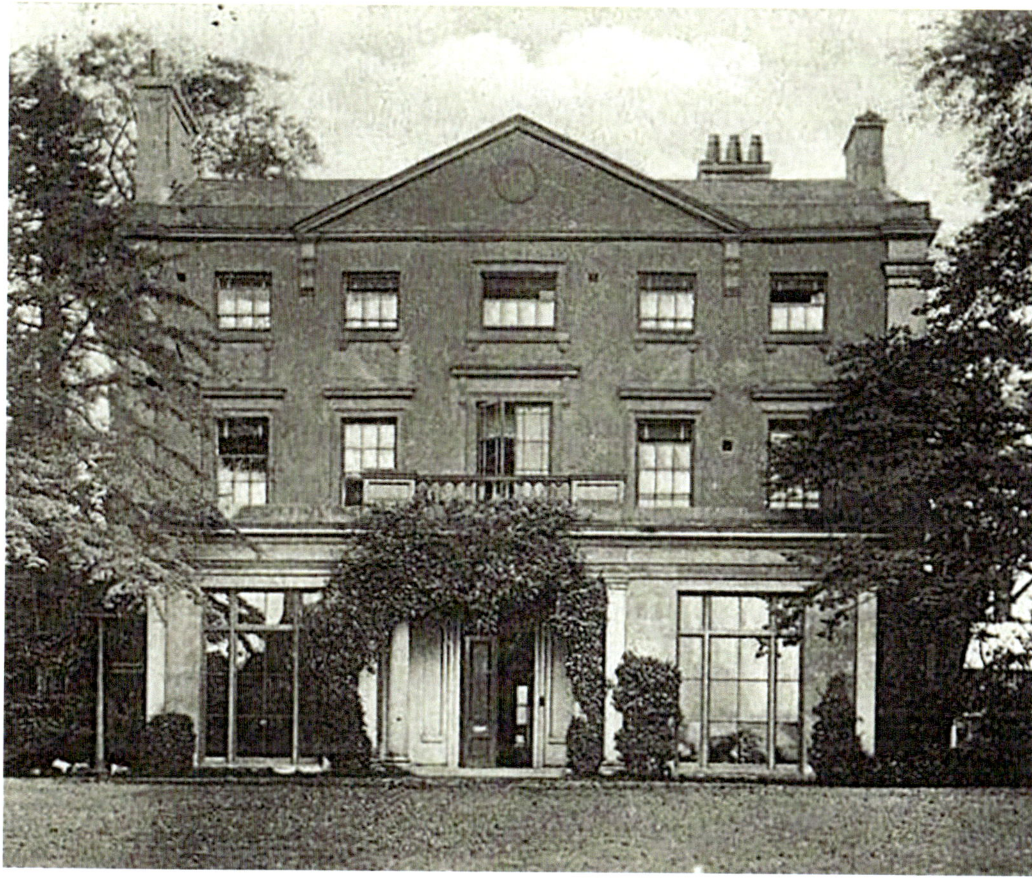

Bournbrook Hall's entrance front, *c.* 1904, from a postcard, and there called Bournville Hall. (James Darwin)

sports pavilion being constructed on its lawn. The house itself was demolished around 1907, its associated home farm is now the Old Farm Hotel and its late eighteenth-century stables and walled garden also survive. It was latterly known as Bournville Hall.

28. Corbyn's Hall, Kingswinford, Staffordshire. *c.* 1908

Thomas Corbin was the first recorded holder of land here, in 1286, and his descendant William Corbin was granted more in 1577. In the Civil War it was home to Royalist Lt Henry Baggeley, who fought at Naseby, when it was recorded as Corbyn's Hall. Thomas Corbyn of Hall End sold the 'ancient mansion' and estate to John Hodgetts, who in the 1779 sold it on to the Gibbons family, local ironmasters and later bankers. The house was probably an early eighteenth-century re-casing of the earlier house. Its seven-bay principal façade had three wide gables masquerading as pediments, the central, recessed, one with Diocletian windows and the flanking ones with *oeils-de-boeuf*. The garden front was largely unaltered from the early seventeenth century, being stone built with attic gables. Thomas

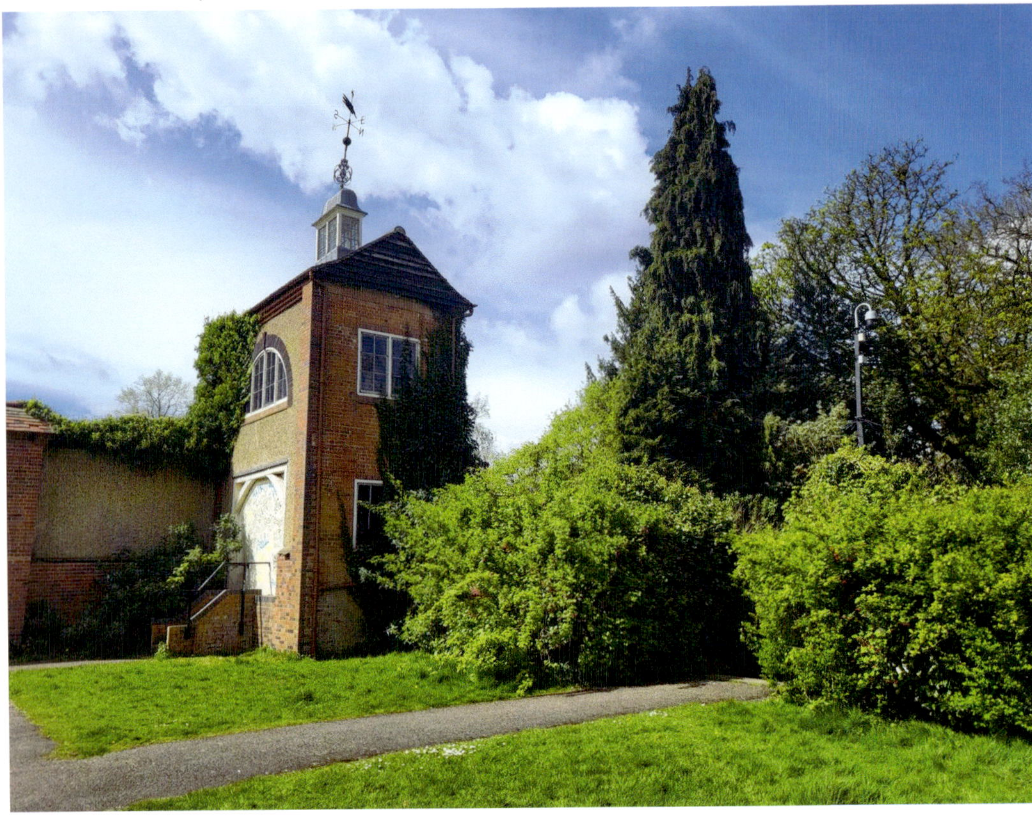

Bournbrook Hall's surviving portion of the stable block, 2019. (Private collection)

Gibbons (b. 1730) developed the estate for mining and built iron foundries but let the house to the Glazebrook family in the 1820s. Benjamin Gibbons was in residence a decade later. By the 1880s the area had become heavily industrialised, and the house was in poor repair. It appears to have been subdivided as tenements at that stage but was subsequently demolished in the Edwardian period to enable redevelopment.

29. Erdington Hall, Erdington, Warwickshire. 1912

The estate was sold to Sir Thomas Holte of Aston Hall in 1647, who let it to ironmaster John Jenyns, whose son Humphrey built the brick house in 1662. It was of brick with stone dressings topped by shaped gables, on a site protected on three sides by a double moat and on the fourth by the River Tame. Jenyns, whose posterity were still in residence in the early eighteenth century, but soon decamped to Gopsal Hall, Leicestershire, letting the house, a later eighteenth-century tenant being Sir Charles Holte, who enlarged the house in 1782, despite having succeeded to the Aston estate in 1770. Soon after, however, the Birmingham to Fazeley Canal was cut through its land and the estate was sold by the Holtes in 1817. It later became the home of the Wheelwrights, who were local farmers, but

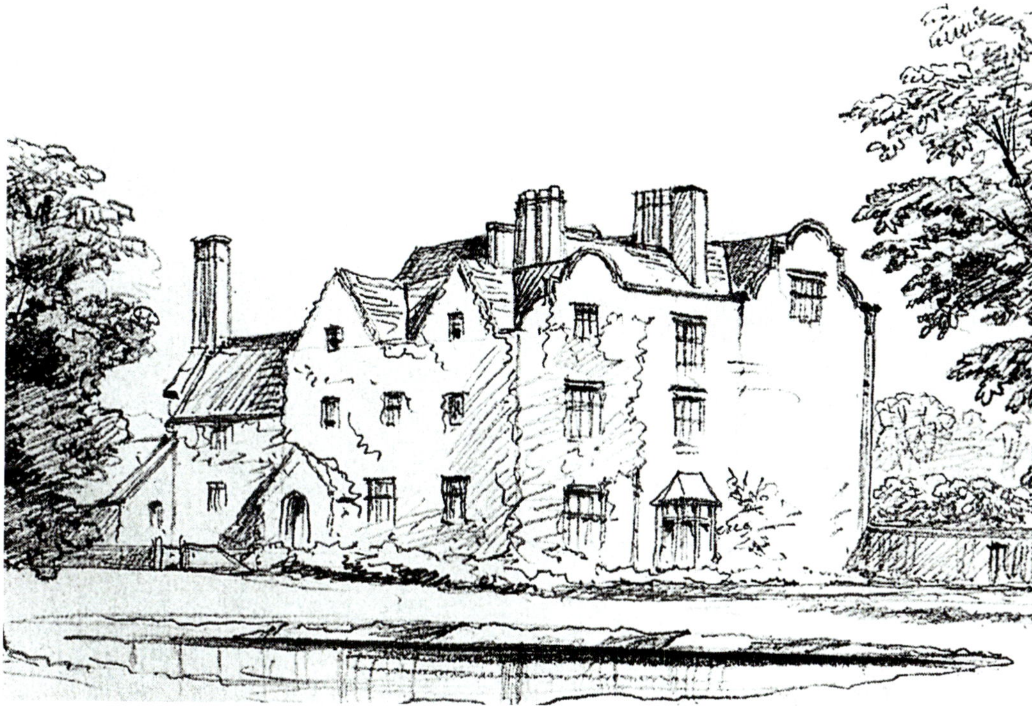

Erdington Hall after a drawing by A. E. Everitt. (Birmingham Museums)

it was demolished *c.* 1912 and its site developed for housing, although Douglas Jones' *History of Erdington* suggests that at least part of the house survived until after the First World War.

30. Turl's Hill House, Sedgley, Staffordshire. *c.* 1920

The first house on this site was built by the Persehouse family in the sixteenth century, followed by the Turleys (hence, presumably, the name). Some parts of this earlier building were incorporated in the nineteenth-century house built by Robert Ebbels (*c.* 1790–1860) in 1848–49 for H. B. Whitehouse. It was a largely early to mid-nineteenth-century brick-built neo-Tudor mansion with stone dressings, which retained parts of the much earlier building. It was occupied by Benjamin Whitehouse (1833–1913) in the 1880s, a member of an important family of ironmasters in the Black Country and proprietor of the Priorfield Furnaces, Deepfield. After their time, it was renamed Wallbrook House and let to Herbert Robinson, a chemicals manufacturer. It was home to a group of Belgian refugees during the First World War but was demolished about 1920.

31. Toll End Hall, Tipton, Staffordshire. *c.* 1922

A remarkable brick Gothic house of 1824 (Hackwood's date) intended for the local ironworks manager which was possibly designed by Samuel Cookson and utilised patterns for the cast-iron windows of a neighbouring church. However, by 1840 it was the home of the works' proprietor, Hollis Solly (1777–1851),

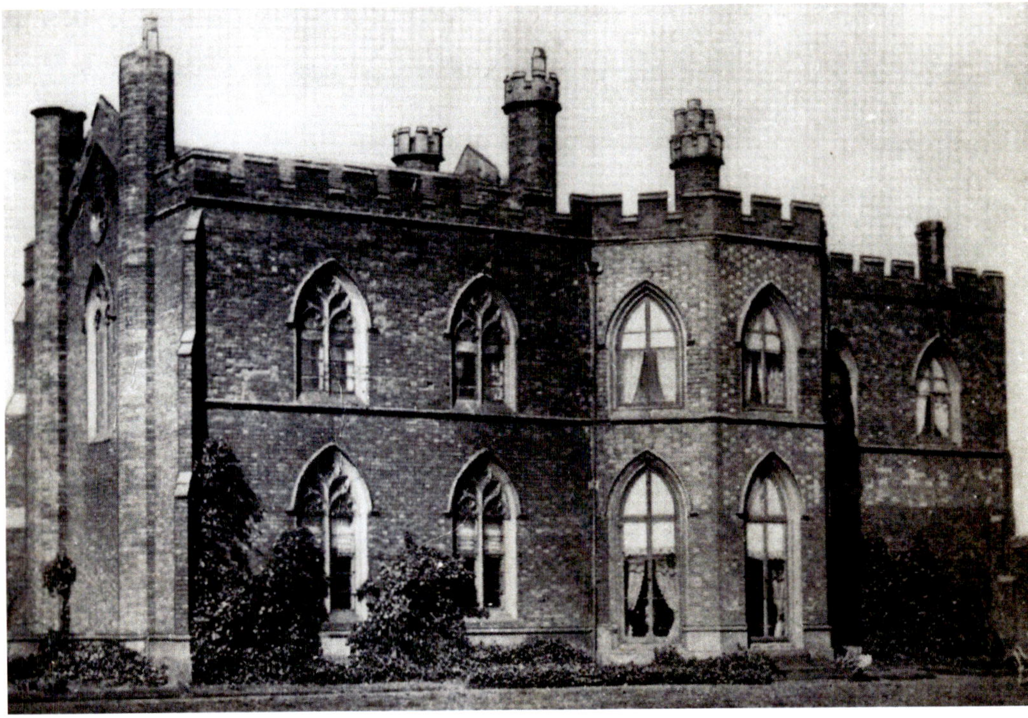

Toll End Hall, *c.* 1900, from Briscoe. (James Darwin)

and his wife Charlotte (née Harrison), the Sollys being descended from Isaac Solly, a wealthy Baltic timber merchant who had first come to the area not long before. Solly was drowned at Porthmadog in July 1851, being succeeded by his opulent son James Hollis Solly. He employed 220 men at his Great Bridge Iron and Steel Company; his brother Richard and his family were also living in the house. James and his wife Caroline extended the house in a similar style, albeit without the fine cast-iron traceried windows of the original range. In the late nineteenth century William Hackwood wrote, in his *Annals of Willenhall*, 'The drawing room and the dining room are lofty apartments with fittings carried out in the ecclesiastical style to the minutest detail … the whole apartment has the appearance of a vestry interior.' The Sollys are not recorded there after 1881, having moved to Edgbaston, when the house is listed as No. 116 Toll End Road, by which time, in any case, the area had become urbanised. It limped on, first let and then as offices before being cleared after the First World War for industrial expansion.

32. Low Hill House, Bushbury, Staffordshire. 1923

Low Hill was originally built, it is said, around 1760 as a plain brick two-storey villa for Willis Kempson, whose son, Revd Gough Willis Kempson, sold it in 1794 to George Pountney, a Wolverhampton banker, who rebuilt it in the first decade of the new century, endowing it with pilasters, parapet, pediment, service

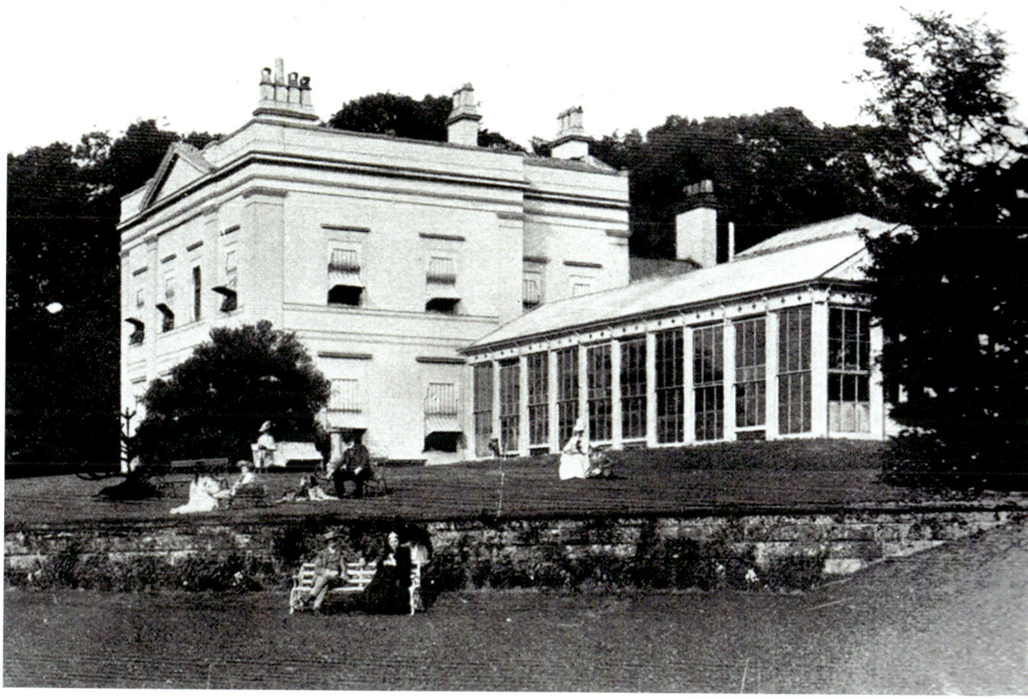

Low Hill House from the east, *c.* 1900, from Briscoe. (James Darwin)

wing, a ten-bay conservatory and covering the house in Roman cement. The son, Richard Savage Pountney, died in 1838 when it passed to John Pountney, who died in 1850. It thereafter became the home of the Norton family, owners of Wolverhampton's Steam Mill but, in 1872, it was again sold, this time to Henry Lovatt, a prosperous civil engineer and contractor who also had a mansion in Oxfordshire. The Lovatts sold the house's contents in 1907. A year later Lovatt's widow Emma sold a lease of the stables and coach house and much of the land, followed by the freehold in 1915. It was demolished in 1923 to make way for an estate of municipal housing.

33. Bradley Hall, Kingswinford, Staffordshire. 1924

Bradley Hall was a timber-framed house of two storeys and attics, originally probably E-plan but, as latterly surviving, with only one projecting end gable, jettied over a canted bay, and a tri-gabled full-height projecting porch. The east end of the building had been rebuilt in stone *c.* 1689 to house a Catholic domestic chapel. The estate came into the family of Hoo by 1525, the house being built by Anthony Hoo (d. 1614) in 1596 (dated on the bressumer of the ground floor south-west window) and had a particularly fine oak staircase. John Hoo of Bradley, Serjeant at Law (1659–1720), purchased an estate at Wednesbury and his nephew and heir John was of Great Barr, so the old house was long in the tenancy of the Dickinsons. In 1801 the estate was held by two heiresses, Mrs Edward

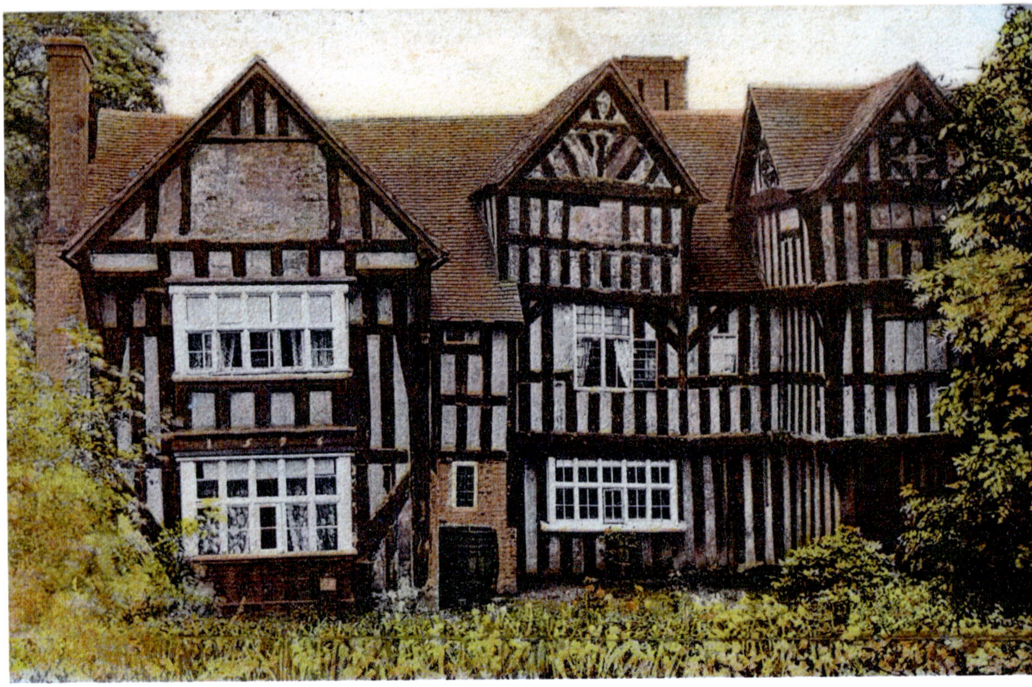

Bradley Hall, *c.* 1913, from a lithographic postcard. (M. Craven)

Whitby and Hon. Mrs Edward Foley, whose tenant in 1801 was eighty-year-old Richard Taylor, a farmer. After changing hands several times in the nineteenth century, it was abandoned after the First World War and owner Henry Webb, butcher and farmer, sold it in 1923 to A. H. Guest of Stourbridge, who dismantled it the following year and used much of the framing to build a new house, Bradley Lodge (now The Grange), on the outskirts of Stratford-upon-Avon.

34. Dunstall Hall, Wolverhampton, Staffordshire. *c.* 1925

John de Hampton held the estate at Dunstall in 1331 and his family remained until in 1530, when the heiress married Richard Waller of Oldstock, who in 1562 sold the estate to John Rivers and from him it passed to Humphrey Moseley fourteen years later, who rebuilt the ancient manor house on its moated platform, adding a three-storey gabled brick gatehouse plastered with Latin mottoes. In 1642 Francis Wightwick acquired the estate, whose posterity partly recased the house in brick in the 1730s. Before 1801, John Wightwick had let the house to a Mr Miller, who, Stebbing Shaw assures us, was a 'very intelligent farmer'. However, the house was greatly enlarged and largely rebuilt in a restrained neo-Tudor style in 1829 for Henry Hill (d. 1870), probably by Francis Goodwin, who certainly designed a lodge there. Inevitably, the setting of the house was impaired in the late 1840s by the building of the Shrewsbury & Birmingham Railway and its workshops, further harm being inflicted by the workshops' enlargement *c.* 1870. Hill's son Sir Alexander Steveley Hill QC, MP soldiered on there until 1889, when he retired to Oxley Hall (q.v.) having overseen the founding of Wolverhampton Racecourse

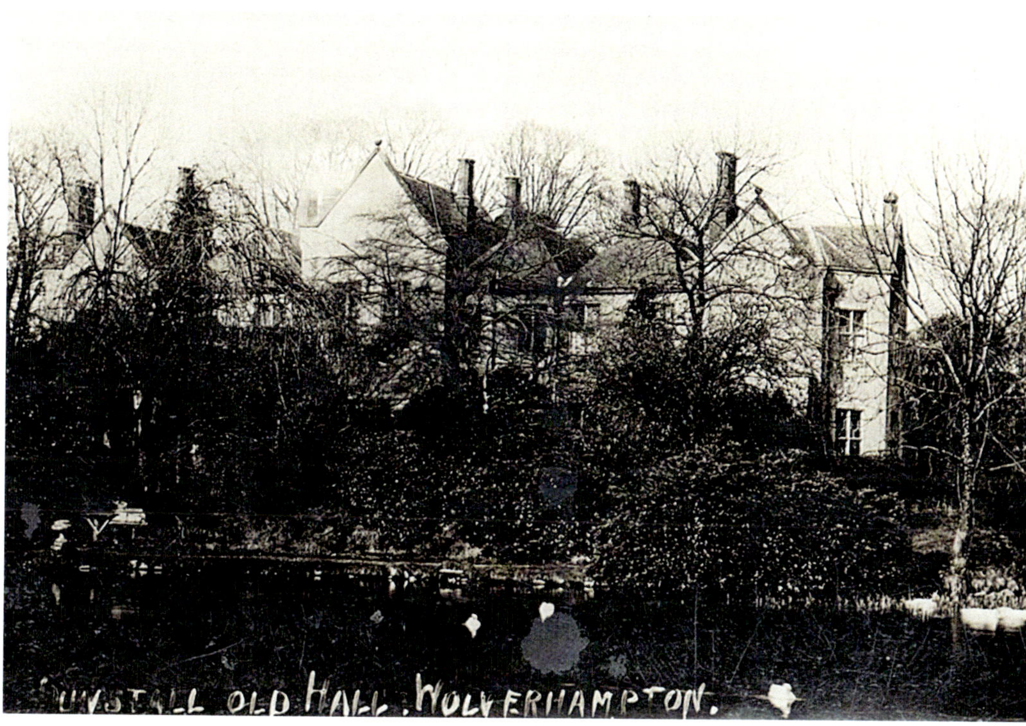

Dunstall Hall, 1913, from a postcard. (M. Craven)

in the remaining grounds, which opened on 13 August 1888. By the time of its demolition in 1915, the mansion was a roofless shell, whilst its impressive gatehouse lingered on until about 1925.

35. Wollaston Hall, Stourbridge, Worcestershire. 1926

This substantial timber-framed early seventeenth-century mansion was acquired by merchant taylor George Liddeatt in 1592, who seems to have built the house. His posterity sold in 1672 to Thomas Foley and it was mainly thereafter let until 1848, the Homfray family, ironmasters, being the principal tenants. John Homfray (1759–1837) assumed the surname and arms of Addenbrooke on inheriting The Lea in 1792. In 1826, however, the freehold was purchased by the 1st Earl of Dudley, but in 1848 their Himley estate sold, and Wollaston was acquired by William Blow Collis. It was again sold in 1859, on this occasion to Henry Onions Firmstone, around which time the house was altered, Firmstone probably adding a stone, three-storey, crenellated range with mullioned windows set beneath hood moulds. Some of the timber framing appearing on historic photographs of the side elevations also looks suspiciously like decorative cladding of about that date. The last occupier of the house was Caleb Roberts, who died in 1918. Its contents were sold by his daughter in 1924 and the house was demolished in 1926, much of the timber fabric being sold to American clients; panelling and a fireplace survive at Ford House, Gaukler Pointe, Detroit, built in 1926–29 for Edsel, son of Henry Ford.

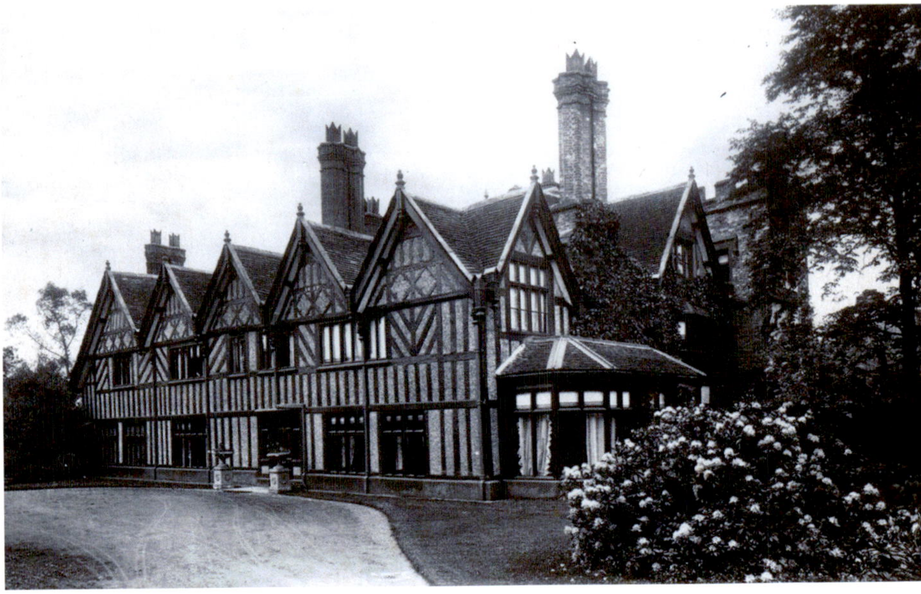

Wollaston Hall, *c.* 1900, from a postcard. (James Darwin)

36. Perry Hall, Perry Barr, Staffordshire. 1927

Perry Hall was in Staffordshire until 1928, held by the de Perry family from Domesday Book times until eventually it passed to Eustace FitzHerbert, whose heiress brought it to Thomas Smith. He sold to Judge William Stamford, who built a new L-plan house of some distinction within the old moat, dated 1576. Royalist Edward Stamford was ruined in the Civil War, and the estate was disposed of

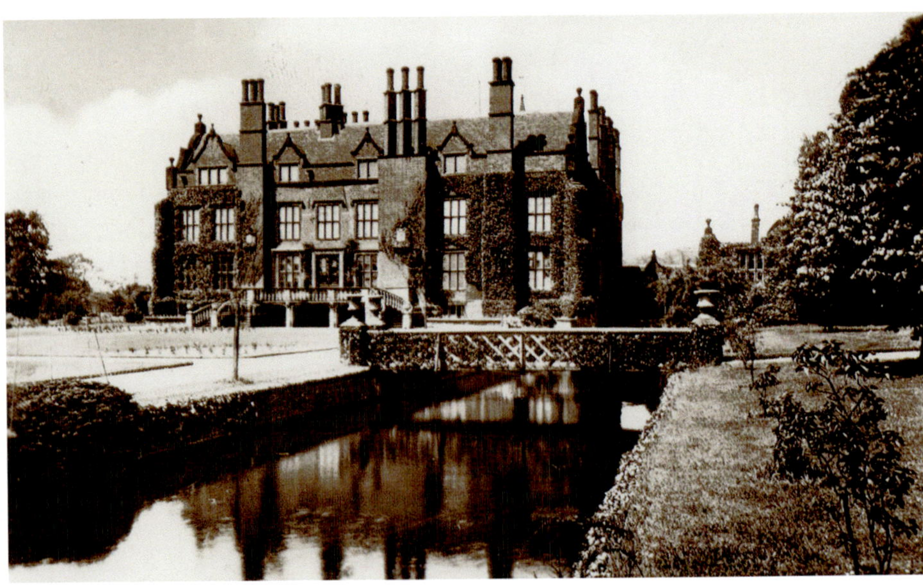

Perry Hall as rebuilt, from a postcard of *c.* 1906. (M. Craven)

to Richard Best, who sold it in 1669 to Sir Henry Gough, son of John Gough of Oldfallings, Bushbury, and of a family of Wolverhampton merchants of The Staple. He improved the old house with cross windows and an enclosed courtyard. The senior male line died out with the death of John Gough (1780–1844) when it became the property of a collateral line, the Gough Calthorpes, later Lords Calthorpe, Lt Gen. 7th Lord Calthorpe KCB having been resident there until he succeeded in 1910. He died two years later. The family rebuilt the house 1842–45, greatly enlarging with an extra wing and refronting it, the architect for which is not known. The Birmingham architect H. R. Yeoville Thomason, however, undertook work here *c.* 1872. The family ceased to live there in 1919, whereupon it was sold to Birmingham Corporation with 500 acres of land for new housing, the old house being pulled down in 1927. Inexplicably, the moat was filled in 1934 and a new smaller one excavated. The stables went in 1935.

37. Heathfield Hall, Handsworth, Staffordshire. 1927

In 1790, on the recommendation of his partner, Matthew Boulton, James Watt commissioned Samuel Wyatt to build him a villa at Heathfield, but whilst the drawings exist, the house into which he actually moved was less stylish – of two storeys, two five-bay cross wings being separated by a lower central range with a cupola set back and curved, and bays to the north, all stuccoed – into which he moved in 1791. It was equipped with all the clever devices of domestic economy that were evolving under the inventive Lunar Society coterie of which Watt was a member: flushing closets, back boilers heating water, efficient heating and ventilation systems, as at Soho House and Sycamore House (q.v.). The park extended to 40 acres and Watt's workshop was above the three-storey service wing, which was sealed on his death in 1819. The family retained the house after

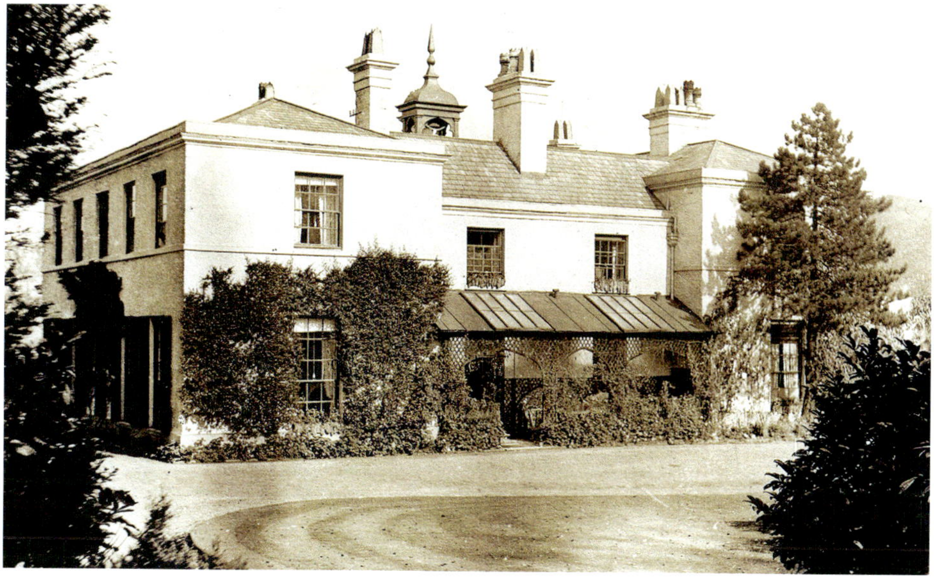

Heathfield House, 1908, from a postcard. (James Darwin)

the death of Watt's son in 1848, beginning the disposal of the land for development in 1874 and letting it in 1880 to manufacturer George Tangye, who died there in 1920. Watt's great-grandson J. M. Gibson Watt decided to sell and in 1924 gave the content of the attic workshop to the Science Museum and sold the remainder of the contents. The house went for redevelopment and was demolished in 1927.

38. Stivichall Hall, Coventry, Warwickshire. 1928

Thomas Gregory, town clerk of Coventry, bought land at Styvechale in 1582 from the Ferrers of Tamworth and a house there by marriage with the Wades. Arthur Gregory replaced the house in 1755–60 to the designs of Henry Flitcroft but the interior was not completed until *c.* 1770. It was an ashlar three-storey structure over a semi-basement, five bays wide, the central pedimented bay breaking forward with a first-floor Venetian window beneath a thermal one, all flanked by matching three-bay pavilions attached by single-storey links with a further, smaller pair beyond – a very stylish Palladian set-piece. The interior contained chimneypieces carved by Joseph Pickford and Richard Hayward. The next generation saw the simplification of the pavilions and the provision of a matching full-height extension to the east. The hall was sold in 1928 by Maj. C. H. Gregory-Hood and was demolished in stages after the sale of the estate in 1932. It finally disappeared soon after the Second World War. An icehouse in the garden and a stable court to the south-east survived for a few more years. In 1964, although the site was still vacant, no buildings were left, and the former gardens were derelict and overgrown.

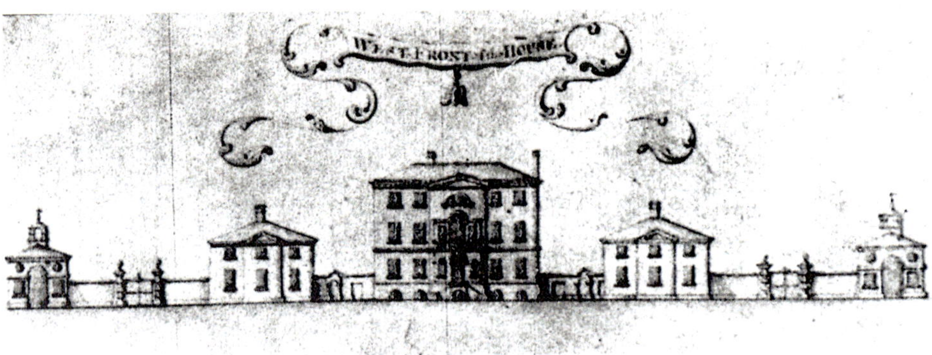

Stivichall Hall in 1775 after a survey by William Roe, from R. Bearman (1972). (Private collection)

39. Sandwell Park, West Bromwich, Staffordshire. 1928

Sandwell was the site of a Benedictine priory, which was granted to Cardinal Wolsey in 1536 but came from him to Lady Lucy Clifford, whose grandson sold in 1569 to Robert Whorwood. In 1701 Thomas Brome Whorwood sold the estate to William Legge, 2nd Lord Dartmouth (later 1st Earl), who commissioned William Smith of Warwick to build a new stone house in 1705–11. This was of two storeys with attic dormers and a nine-bay façade. In around 1771 the 2nd Earl had Timothy Lightoler add Palladian pyramid-capped, three-storey,

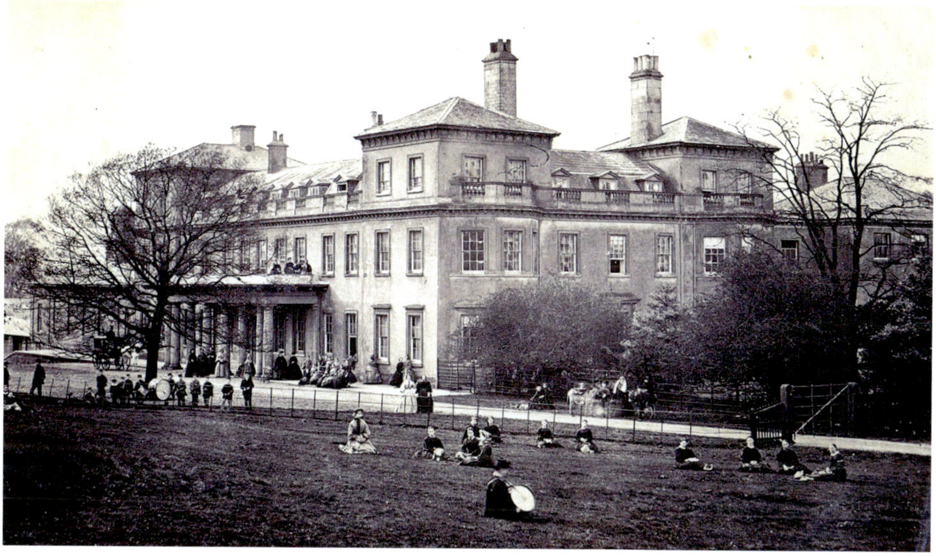

Sandwell Hall in the 1880s, whilst in use as a school. (James Darwin)

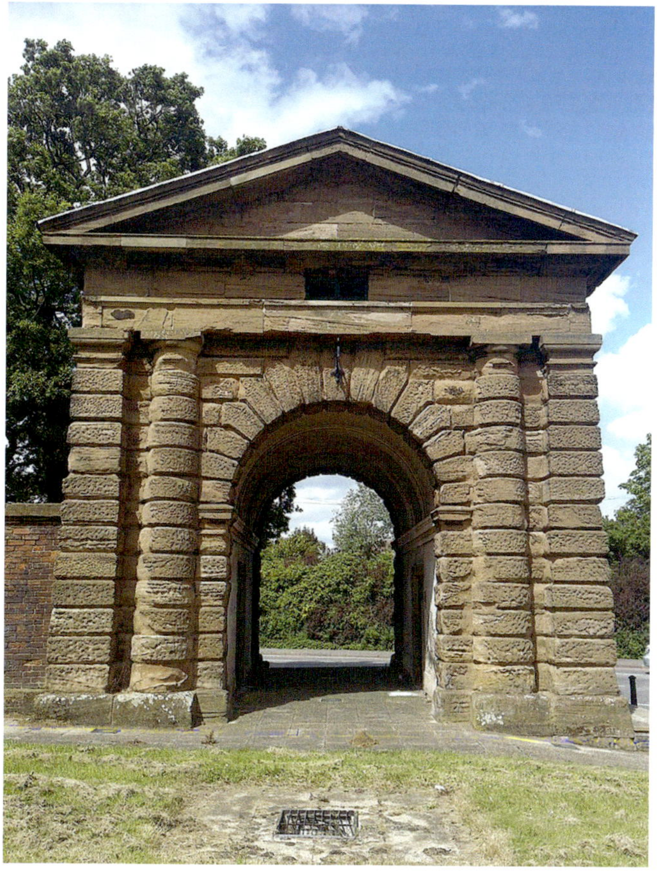

Sandwell Hall's surviving lodge portico, 2021. (M. Craven)

two-bay towers at the angles with canted bays to the returns. Around 1800 Henry Hakewill repositioned the chimneys crowning the corner pavilions, whilst from 1822 Thomas Rickman made additions for the 4th Earl, including an octostyle Tuscan portico. In 1853 the Dartmouths moved to Patshull and let the house to George Muntz MP, then from 1857 to a variety of benevolent institutions (selling the freehold in 1913) until the last one closed in 1921, by which time the house had become fatally compromised by mining subsidence and it was cleared – 'no great loss' in the opinion of the late Professor Gomme – in 1928. An extraordinary Vanbrugh-esque lodge survives in the middle of a nearby traffic island.

40. Moor Green Hall, Moseley, Warwickshire. 1928

Moor Green Hall was a two-storey villa of brick and stucco with mildly Gothic four-centered, arched windows and low battlements, which appears to have gained a further extension a generation later, tricked out in matching style. There was also an attached stable block which stood within a substantial wooded park. It may have been built for James Taylor of the Moseley Hall family. It appears on the 1840 Tithe Map when the estate was occupied by Sarah Taylor. The estate was leased by the Chamberlain family during the second half of the nineteenth century, its occupiers including Foreign Secretary Sir Austen Chamberlain KG PC MP (1863–1937). The last of the Chamberlains to live there was Arthur Chamberlain, brother of Joseph and director of the Birmingham firm of Chamberlain and Hookham, who died in Devon in October 1913. The house became a military hospital during the First World War, but failed to find a use thereafter, being demolished in 1928.

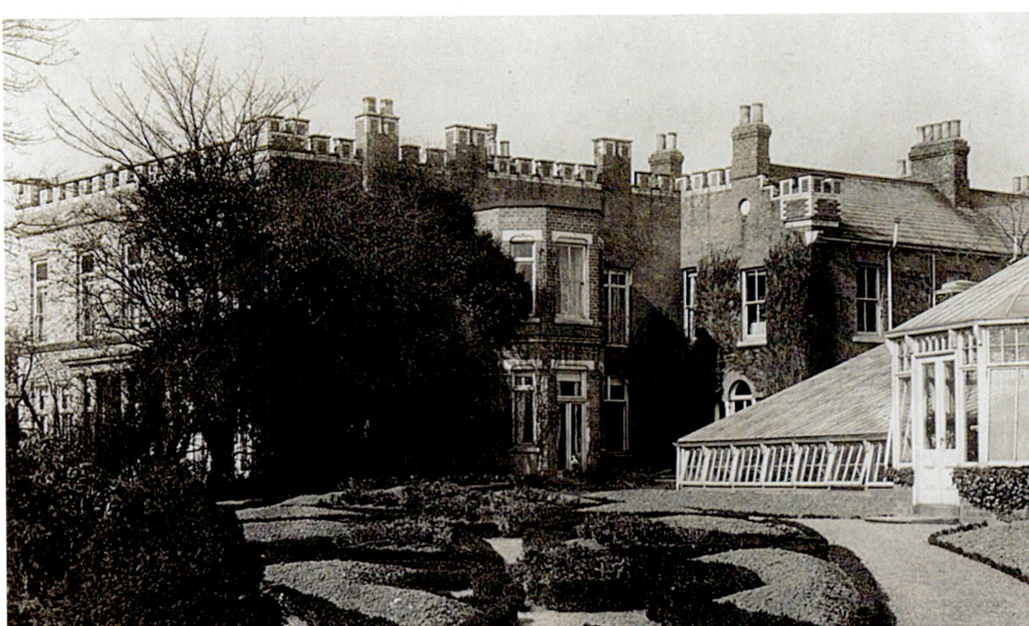

Moor Green Hall from the east, from a postcard of *c.* 1906. (M. Craven)

41. Bentley Hall, Willenhall, Staffordshire. 1929

The Lanes succeeded the Hillary family at Bentley in 1438. Thomas Lane (d. 1588) was owner of Bentley Hall in 1580, when the house was burnt in a violent dispute over common rights. The following year he replaced it with new E-plan brick house embellished with crowstepped gables and later a pretty Bach y Graig-style detached banqueting house was added. In 1651 Col John Lane and his sister found fame hiding Charles II there after the Battle of Worcester. Fifteen years later they were taxed on fourteen hearths. In the early eighteenth century, the house was drastically reduced and rebuilt in red brick, including a very handsome entrance front of two storeys with a five-bay façade of arched fenestration, with the east cross wing rebuilt in much plainer style all under a panelled parapet. The estate was sold to the Ansons in 1747 and whilst Edward Anson was still in residence in the early 1830s, the contents were sold on his death in 1836.

It was later owned by S. H. Walker and in 1908 farmed by William Longmore, but the structure became dangerous due to mining subsidence, and it was vacated and in 1929 demolished. Its site was marked by a cairn in 1935, erected by the local council.

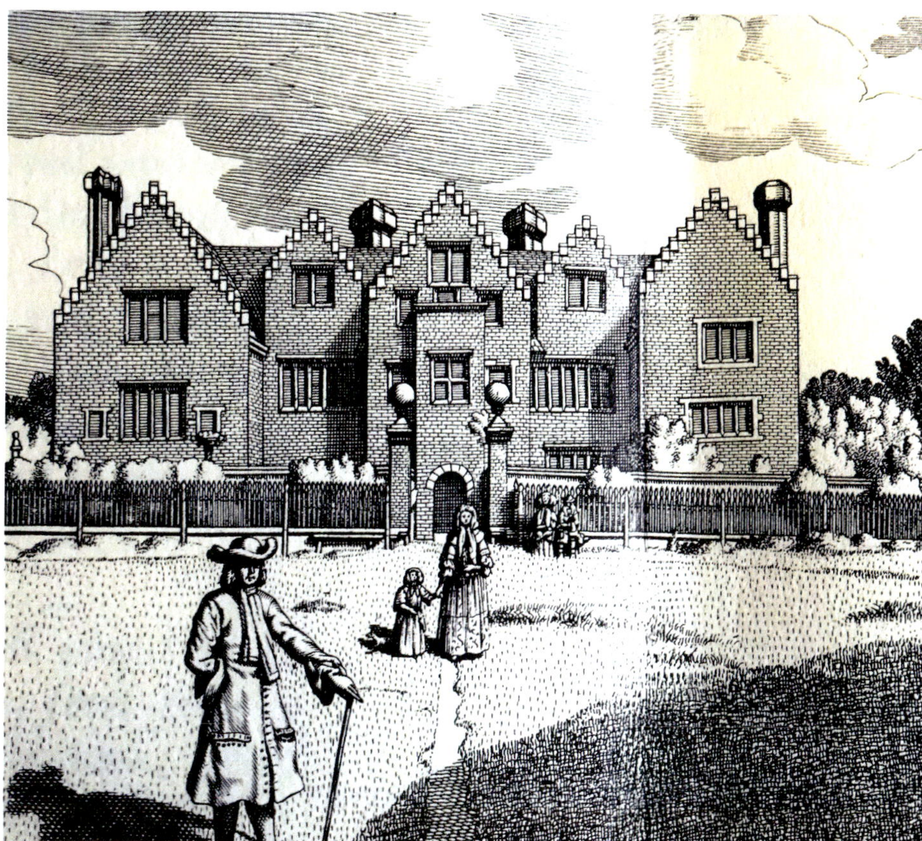

Bentley Hall in 1696 from Dr Plot. (M. Craven)

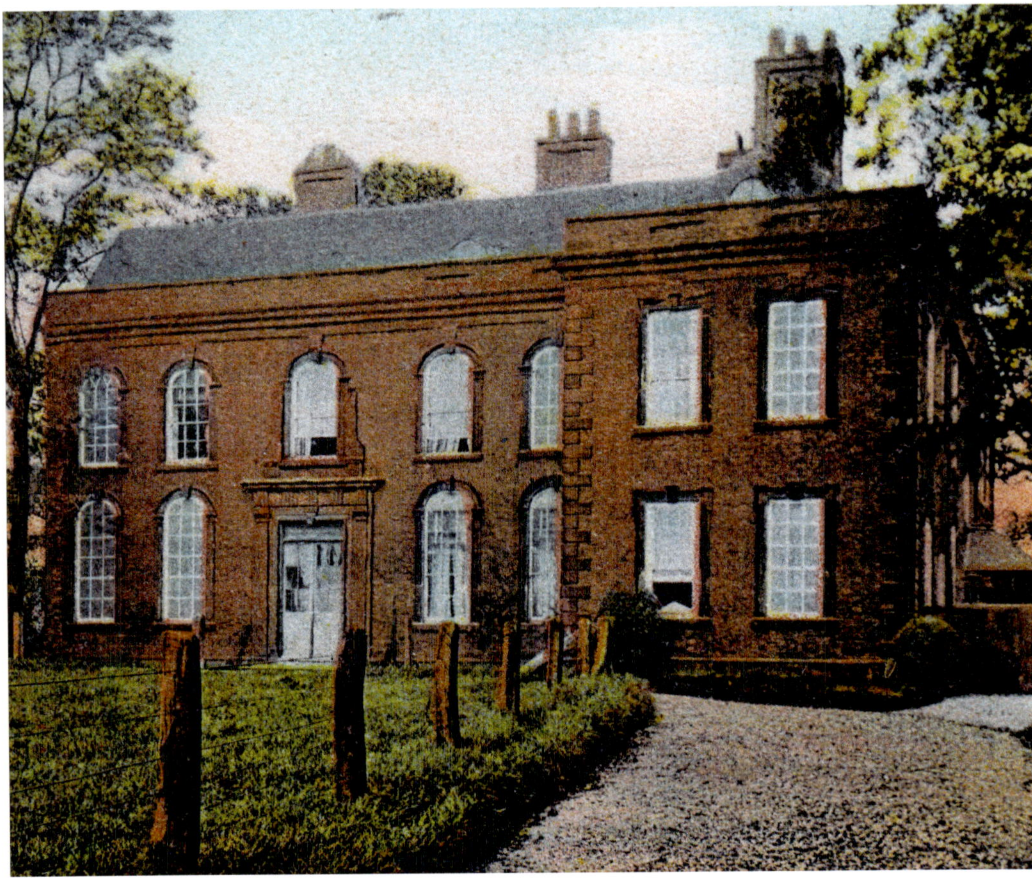

Bentley Hall in 1907, from a postcard. (James Darwin)

42. Oxley Manor, Bushbury, Staffordshire. 1929

The estate was originally owned by the Marnham family, from which it passed to the Derbyshire Lowes and from them to a younger son of Lord Grey of Wilton and thence in 1480 to the Lords Dudley. In 1535 the Greys sold to John Leveson, whose posterity sold it to John Langley, whose descendant Timothy Langley disposed of it in 1761 to the father of William Huskisson of Birtsmorton (1753–90). His son, William Huskisson MP (1770–1830), sold it to Wolverhampton banker James Hordern. The original house was replaced in 1854 by Hordern's son William, who built a substantial gabled, two-storey, asymmetrical neo-Tudor house in diapered red brick and stone dressings to the designs of Ewan Christian, but which incorporated part of the earlier house at its north-western angle. It passed by marriage to the Hills of Dunstall and from 1889 became the home of Sir Alexander Staveley Hill MP after he left Dunstall (q.v.). His son, Lt Col Henry Staveley Hill MP, sold the estate in 1920 after leaving Parliament and moved to London, before eventually settling in Evesham in 1938. By this time, suburban housing was beginning to encroach on the park, and in 1929 it was cleared away.

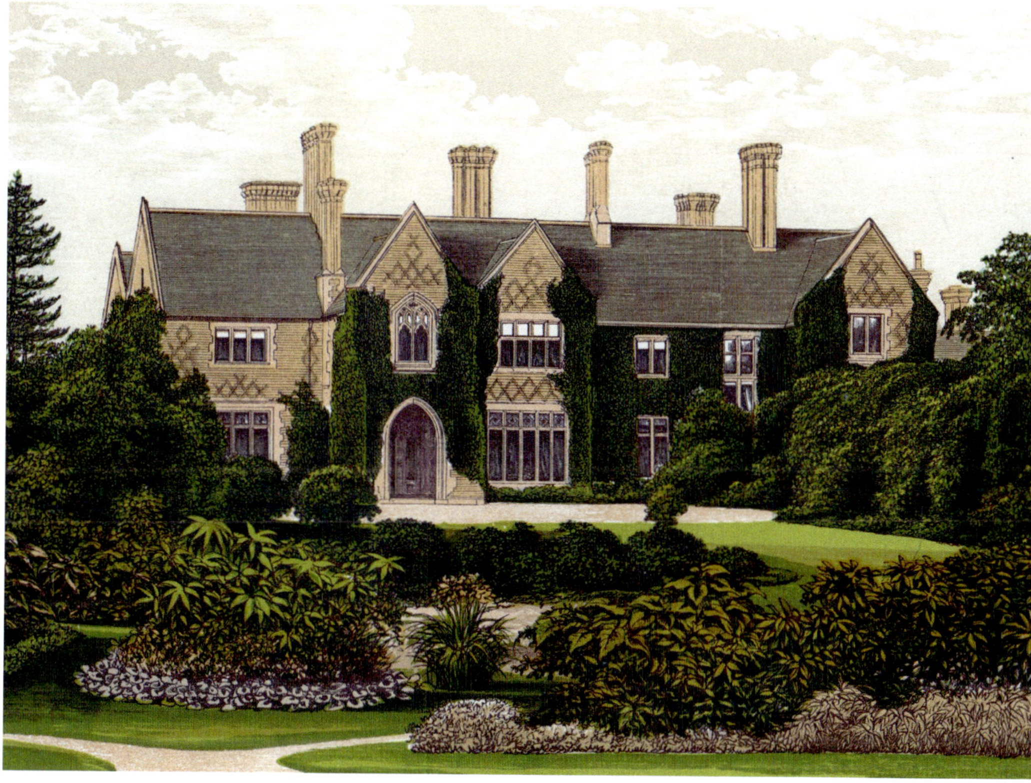

Oxley Manor as rebuilt by Ewen Christian, after F. O. Morris, 1880. (James Darwin)

43. Bennetts Hill House, Washwood Heath, Warwickshire. 1930

Bennetts Hill was built by the irascible historian William Hutton of Red Hill House (q.v.) for his son Thomas at the beginning of the nineteenth century on part of the Red Hill House grounds and who in 1827 had Charles Edge alter the house, adding a Doric loggia, a veranda, a round ground-floor entrance with a domed top, other alterations and adding a coat of Roman cement, causing his sister, the historian and novelist Catherine Hutton (d. 1846) – who inherited the house on his death – to complain, in a surviving letter, of her brother's architectural mania, which 'shows itself in pillars and porticos'. In fact, it was latterly a substantial, stylish if architecturally wayward stuccoed villa of two and three storeys under a broad-eaved hipped roof, the two-storey service wing ending in a bellcote. The entrance hall had a fine ceiling, with richly carved doorcases and a fluted Corinthian screen, within which was an arch forming the entrance to the principal stairs. The doorcase on the garden front was set within a curved urn-capped porch and had a lintel carved with swags, and sported fluted Corinthian columns. By the early twentieth century, parts of its grounds had been sold for housing. The last owner, Mr Herrick, died in 1928, and the house was empty and in an advanced state of decay by the time of its demolition in 1930. The site is now occupied by flats.

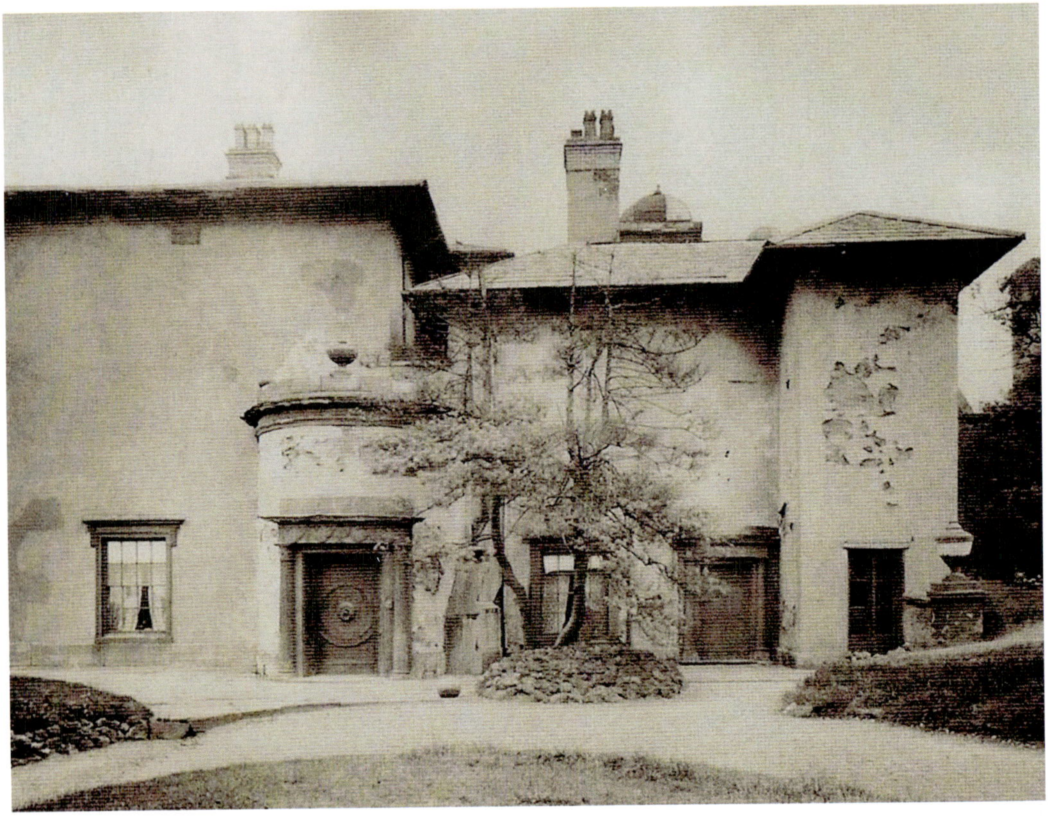

Bennetts Hill House in decay, 1920s. (Private collection)

44. Leveretts (The), Handsworth, Staffordshire. *c.* 1930

The Leveretts was a distinguished three-storey stuccoed classical house which was possibly built for Anthony Ravee, a merchant, around 1790. Ravee obtained a private Act of Parliament to become a British citizen in 1791 and it was in the ownership of his son Henry in the early nineteenth century but soon afterwards let to Richard Jesson, who died there in August 1810. It was then let to ironmaster Samuel Dawes, whose son Henry succeeded him there and the family remained in residence until the early 1830s, although Henry Ravee had died in 1820. The house appears then to have been sold and again in the late nineteenth century, this time to the Sandwell Park Colliery Company, who let it in 1900 to the Windsor Green Asylum as a female psychiatric institution, which closed in 1911 upon moving to the larger Stechford Hall (q.v.). The freehold of the estate was then purchased by Handsworth Urban District Council, and a large section of the grounds became part of Handsworth Cemetery, the house going in around 1930. Its fine twin classical lodges survived another two decades, by which time they were in a ruinous condition.

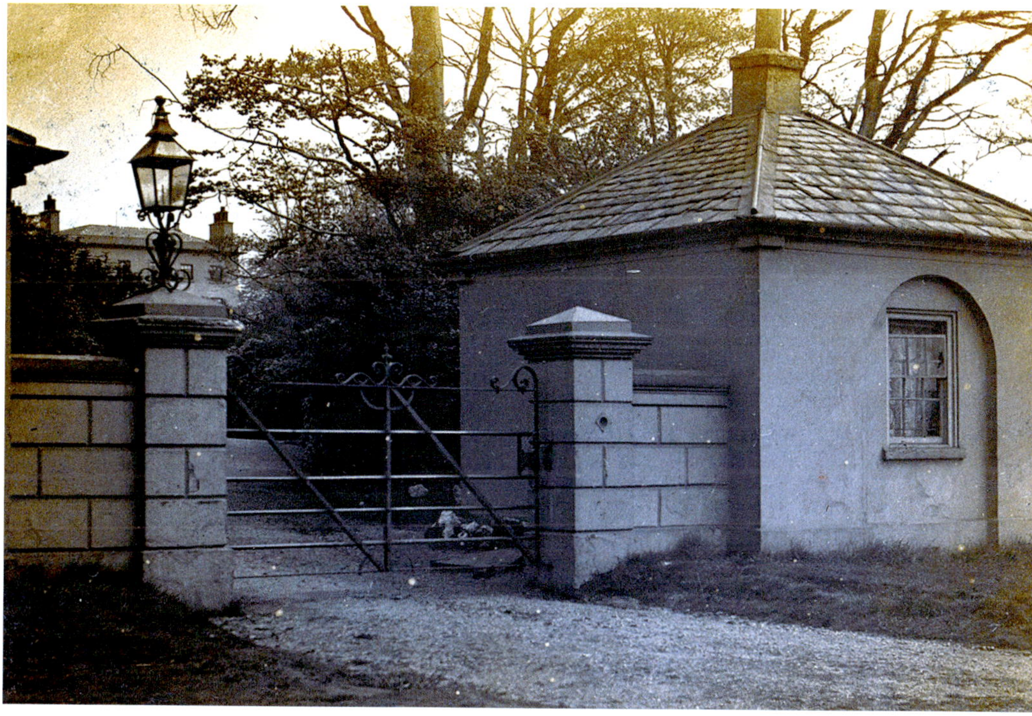

The Leveretts, seen from the lodges on Camp Lane, *c.* 1906, from a postcard. (James Darwin)

45. Hazelwell Hall, Kings Heath, Warwickshire. 1931

On this site once stood a manor house that belonged to the Hazelwelles, which then passed to the Middlemores, whose fortunes declined after the Civil War and, by the early nineteenth century, the estate was let. In 1715, Thomas Middleomre sold the estate to George Birch, who rebuilt the house and let it as a farm, a situation which continued until around 1830. In the late 1830s it was the home of Charles Huskinson, who died here in 1857, and in 1864 Samuel Phillips was the tenant. The house appears to have been of two distinct phases. The earlier part was of two storeys and three bays, forming much of the entrance front and service wing. To this, possibly in the later 1860s, was added a substantial three-storey stone-faced Italianate block with canted bays fronting the gardens. A substantial Italianate porch was also added at around the same time to the entrance front. Charles Edward Bateman is, however, known to have drawn up plans to extend and alter the house for George Cartland QC in 1886. If the additions are his work, then they are of a remarkably conservative design for their date. In the early twentieth century the Cartlands began to develop the estate for housing through the aegis of the Priory Estate Company and the house was used as a convalescent home for wounded soldiers during the First World War. George and Lillian Cartland moved to Henwick Grange, Worcestershire, and the remnants of the estate were developed for housing. The house was demolished in 1931.

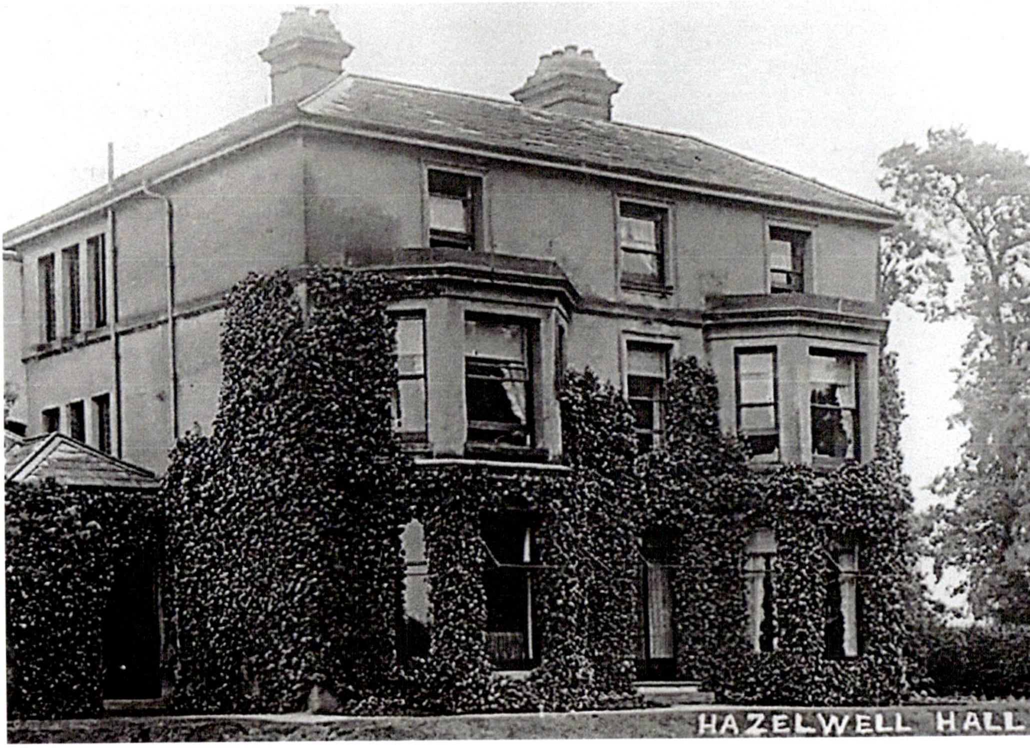

Hazelwell Hall, *c.* 1904, from a postcard. (James Cartland)

46. Wood End House, Erdington, Warwickshire. 1932

Formerly known as Pype Manor House after the family of that name, for part of the nineteenth century it was also called Wood House and Littlewood Hall. It was a highly picturesque timber-framed multi-gabled building which stood adjacent to the moated site of an even earlier mansion. It was said to have been built by John Butler in 1543, but the estate was sold to the Holdens around 1569, who probably built it, and the house was enlarged by Humphrey Holden in 1622 to resemble Wollaston (q.v.) in both scale and proportion and the family retained the freehold into the nineteenth century. At its rear was a range of timber-framed outbuildings. The hall had a fine carved overmantel and seventeenth-century wainscot, as did the study and drawing room, although the library was refitted in the eighteenth century. One bedroom had later eighteenth-century plasterwork. From the 1880s the house, by this time partly stuccoed, was home to Daniel and Sara Causer of the firm Hopkins, Causer & Hopkins. Its gardens were extensive, with a pergola, rock gardens, kitchen gardens and tennis courts. The house was first offered for sale at auction in 1921 but withdrawn because of lack of interest. It was finally sold in October 1931 to a developer from Brighton, this being followed, inevitably, by a demolition sale exactly a year later. The panelling and chimneypieces were not included in this sale, so must have been stripped out and sold before that date.

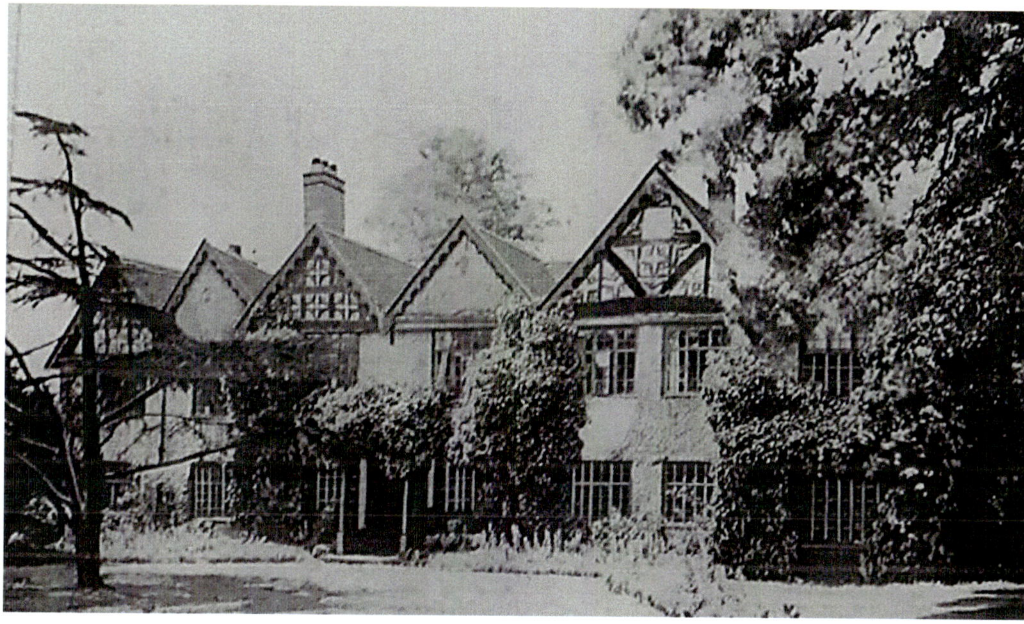

Wood End House at the beginning of the twentieth century, from a postcard. (James Darwin)

47. Stechford Hall, Stechford, Warwickshire. 1932

Stechford Hall was a substantial three-storey, multi-gabled, neo-Tudor brick house with a corner turret designed by J. J. Bateman (1817–1903) for the Birmingham wine merchant Joseph Smallwood in 1863, although an eighteenth-century map by Tomlinson shows a house on the site. Bateman had previously altered a cottage on his estate in 1854 and although a detailed specification for its construction survives, there are no drawings or other correspondence in the Bateman archive. It replaced an earlier house and stood in wooded parkland. The Smallwoods moved away in the late 1880s. The house was later the home of William George Hills, who died in 1903. After that it was let for use as an annexe to All Saints' Mental Hospital to house thirty male patients. The lease ran out in 1932 and the hospital duly closed. The house was demolished, although part of the grounds survive as a 22-acre public park.

48. Whateley Hall, Castle Bromwich, Warwickshire. 1935

This fine stone neoclassical house of *c.* 1797 closely resembles Elmdon Hall (q.v.) and thus could conceivably be by John Standbridge. It later underwent minor mid-nineteenth-century alterations, which stood in a large park with a lake close to the Bradford Arms. It was probably built for the Sadlers. It had a three-storey pedimented ashlar entrance façade with pilasters and a substantial early to mid-nineteenth-century ionic columned porch. The garden façade was stuccoed and much plainer. Until 1856, when he purchased Barrells Hall, it was the seat of William Newton, a linen importer, and they were succeeded after 1862 by Frederick Knight, a paper manufacturer who was living there into the 1880s. It fell into ruin in the mid-twentieth century. Revd William Newton, however, stayed

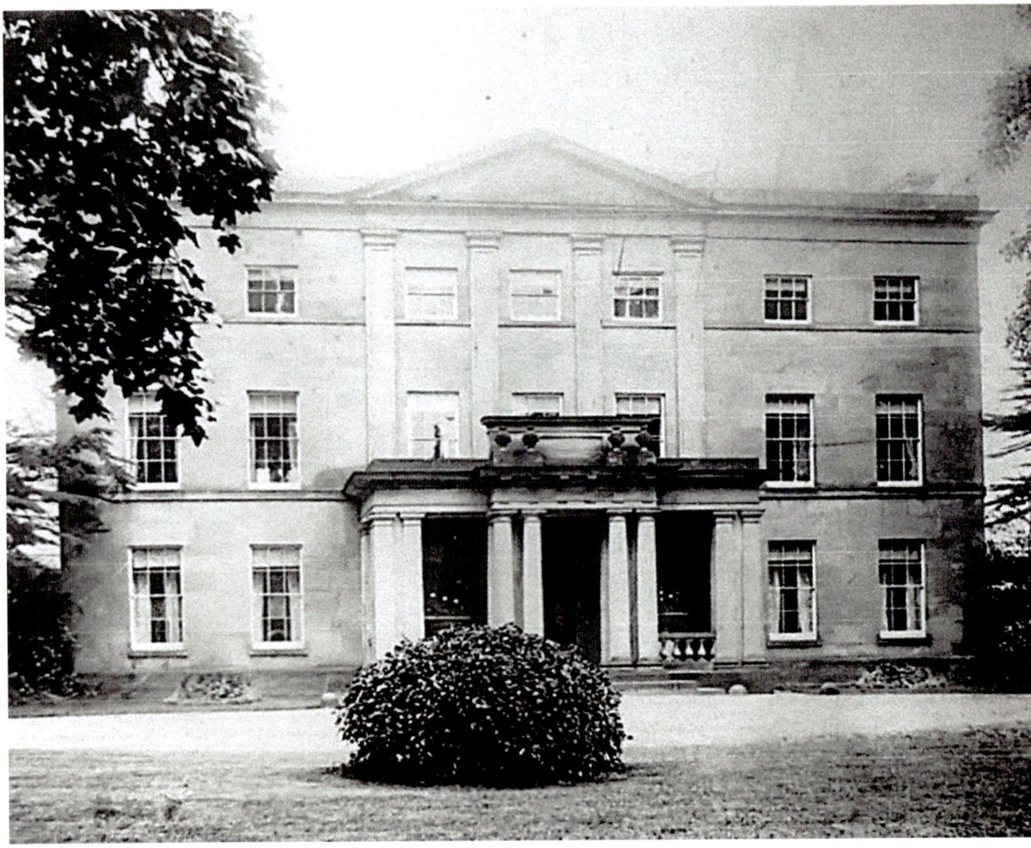

Whateley Hall in the 1890s. (Private collection)

on at Whateley until his death in 1879. From 1881, Whateley Hall was the seat of Frederick Knight of the firm Smith, Stone and Knight, who died at the hall in 1919. Demolished for housing by Hales & Co. of Castle Bromwich, a lodge house survives.

49. Hall Green or Hawe Hall, Hall Green, Worcestershire. *c.* 1936

This house was a low gabled timber-framed structure with a much taller later eighteenth- or early nineteenth-century brick addition, embellished with Gothic cast-iron window frames, an exaggerated Gothic cornice and other minor later nineteenth-century alterations. Whilst extensive timber framing was still visible on the garden façade, the gabled entrance front was almost entirely encased in early to mid-nineteenth-century brick. It was the seat of the Haw family, but in the late eighteenth century, it had been the home of Thomas Edward Dolphin and in the 1830s of Thomas and Elizabeth Steadman. In the mid-nineteenth it was home to John Blakeway. Within Historic England's National Monuments Record collection are two record drawings by Edgar W. Pitt, one showing a section through what appears to be an oval Regency Gothic staircase hall containing an imperial stair, the other showing details of the same room including Gothic

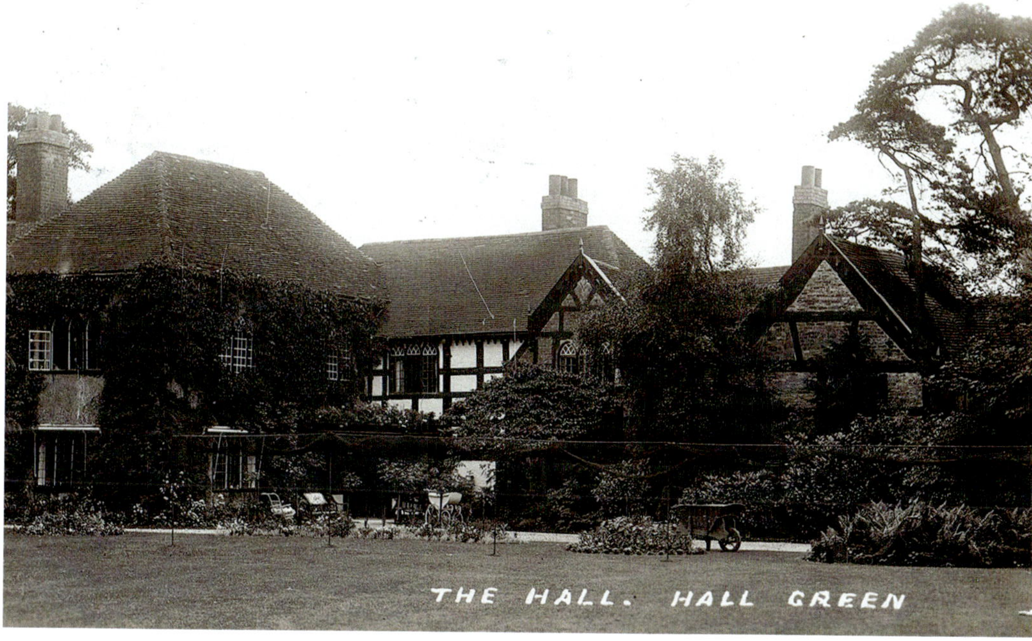

Hall Green Hall's garden front. *c.* 1910. (James Darwin)

plasterwork, plaster reliefs of pelicans and elaborate Gothic doorcases. A fine Dutch, gabled, seventeenth-century home farmhouse home and its outbuildings were also demolished at the same time.

50. Hamstead Hall, Handsworth, Staffordshire. 1936

The Wyrleys held at Hamstead from 1340 and a new Hamstead Hall was built by Sir John Wyrley in 1690, some five years prior to his death without issue. His heiress brought the estate to the Birch family and Humphrey Birch assumed the surname and arms of Wyrley, enlarging the house in 1735. It passed to a cousin, George Birch, who rebuilt the house further in 1801. Wyrley Birch, the son, sold the bulk of the estate in 1819 to William Legge, 4th Earl of Dartmouth. The two-storey house stood in a small park which stretched to the River Tame. Its entrance façade was of five bays with a central pedimented breakfront with a nine-bay return to the south, the end three bays both breaking forward under pediments with thermal windows.

Within, the simple but elegant principal staircase would also have appeared to date from George Birch's rebuilding, as did the fine white marble chimneypieces in the principal reception rooms. The house was let by the Legges, being occupied by a number of important local figures, including George Kynoch, MP for Aston, and John Lewis Moilliet, a banker and son-in-law of Lunar Society member James Keir. Despite the setting being blighted by coal mining from the 1870s, the tenant a decade later, Charles Kirkham, attempted to operate the pleasure grounds as a public attraction. In 1936 the park was redeveloped for housing and the house destroyed. A fragment of the walled garden and a ruinous icehouse reputedly survive.

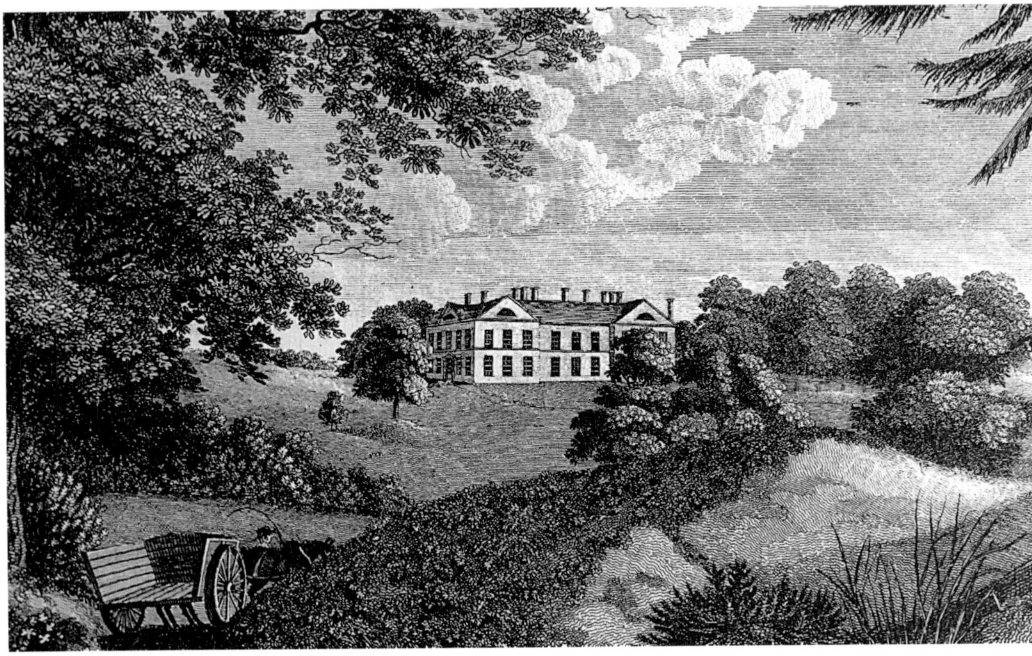

Hamstead Hall in 1801 from Stebbing Shaw. (M. Craven)

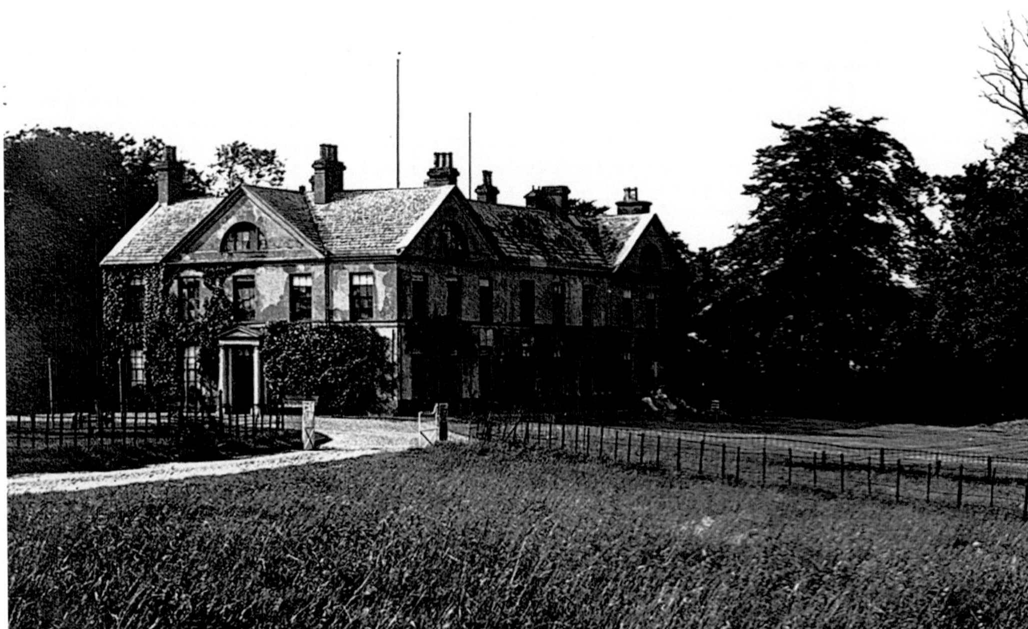

Hamstead Hall, *c.* 1905, from a postcard. (James Darwin)

51. Gilbertstone House, Yardley, Warwickshire. *c.* 1937

A substantial neo-Tudor mansion with diapered brickwork, mullioned windows and a central crenellated octagonal tower was built in 1867–70. The design was the last of three separate schemes of increasing opulence produced by John James Bateman and Benjamin Corser for the wealthy paint and varnish manufacturer Samuel Thornley. The builders were Samuel and William Briggs of Bradford Street, Birmingham. The Thornleys had lived on the estate since at least the 1830s, gradually expanding it through a programme of buying up the surrounding farms, and by the mid-1840s they were laying out a park and commissioning designs for lodges. The grounds straddled the border between the historic counties of Warwick and Worcester and contained a fine lake with a rustic bridge. Very little is known about the previous house, described as a 'farmhouse', which must have been demolished around the same time, as during building works the Thornleys rented Sparkbrook House (q.v.). The final scheme was a Gothic diapered brick two-storey house with attics, plentiful gables, chimneys and pinnacles, all set off by a 60-foot (20-metre) octagon tower with crenellations and a stair turret. The principal interiors were robustly Gothic with marble chimneypieces supplied by the Birmingham firm of James Bennett & Sons and elaborate ironwork including the stair's balustrade from Thomas Thomason of the Medieval Metal Works, Birmingham. The estate was sold shortly after Thornley's death in 1883 to the

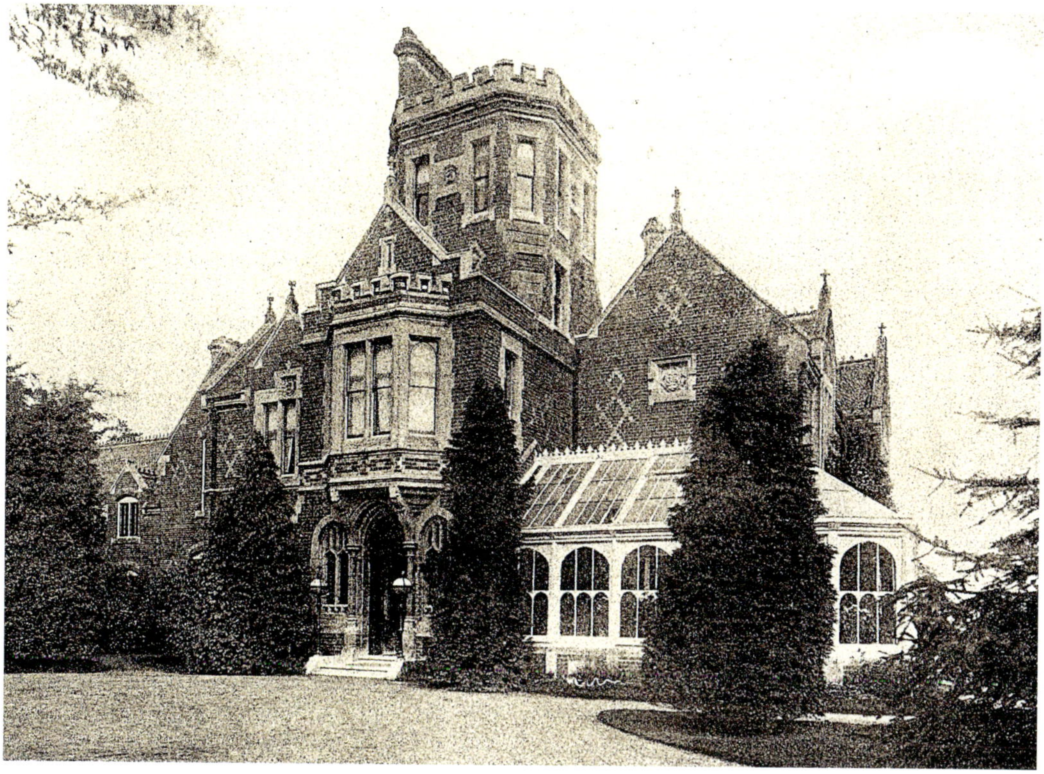

Gilbertstone House's entrance front, 1889. (Birmingham Library)

industrialist Sir Richard Tangye (1833–1906), who internally altered the house, again employing J. J. Bateman, but in 1894 the estate was again sold to George Hookham JP (1843–1924), a former partner of the Chamberlains. The final owner was building contractor and philanthropist Thomas Rowbotham, who began developing outlying portions of the park in the early twentieth century. He died in 1926 and his son Sir Samuel Hanson Rowbotham sold the house and the remainder of the estate for £250,000 in 1936. The house was demolished the following year for building.

52. Smethwick Hall, Smethwick, Staffordshire. 1937

Halesowen Abbey held the manorial estate until 1538 when it was acquired by the Dudleys. A hall had been built by the Restoration, then home of Charles Lane, whose family had probably had it from the Dudleys. Lane later experienced financial difficulties and had sold up by 1702, Henry Hinckley acquiring it. By 1771 it was in the hands of Thomas Hanson (1724–1800), in whose time it became known as Smethwick House, and he seems to have replaced it with a brick three-storey, five-bay villa with a Tuscan portico, rusticated key blocks to the windows, and laid out a small park with a modest lake; the estate ran to 65 acres. Though allegedly built in 1746, a generation later would seem much more likely. The Hansons sold up in 1851 when ironmaster John S. Dawes bought it, but, by 1872, it had been let as a school until 1885 when George Dawes (d. 1888) moved in. In 1890 Sir Richard Tangye of Gilbertstone (q.v.) bought it for his son H. L. Tangye, who later let it. Belgian refugees were housed there from 1914 to 1916 when it was occupied by Benjamin Shakespeare, who left in 1925. The Smethwick Council

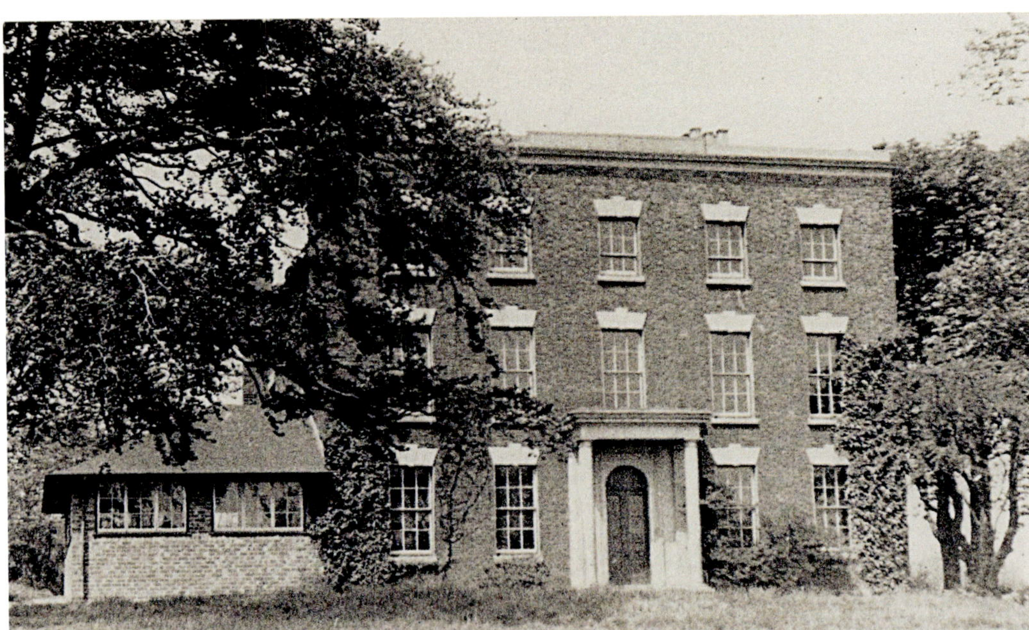

Smethwick Hall, *c.* 1933, from a postcard. (M. Craven)

bought it in 1928 and the remaining grounds became an 8-acre public park. The house was demolished in 1937 and a school built on the site.

53. Fox Hollies Hall, Acocks Green, Worcestershire. *c.* 1937

Originally a substantial farmstead belonging to the Fox family, this house was sufficiently improved in the eighteenth century to become the home of surgeon George Kennedy in the early nineteenth century. The house was partly rebuilt and extended in 1867–70 for Zaccheus Walker III to the designs of H. R. Yeoville Thomason. It thereby gained a rather heavy Italianate air with a campanile and a fine single-storey Italianate side wing with a hipped roof containing an art gallery housing the notable collections of Joseph Walker. The entrance façade was gabled and was entered via an Italianate porch. Yeoville Thomason's surviving June 1869 drawing of the garden elevation shows the picture gallery and tower as built, but with an early nineteenth-century bow window where the canted bay stood. It might seem that the house was again altered therefore by Yeoville Thomason in the 1870s. Col Zaccheus Walker IV began selling the estate in 1925 for development, and the freehold of the house and the remaining land were acquired by Birmingham Corporation with Walker retaining a life interest until his death in 1930. The contents were sold by Christies in July 1933, although the house lingered on until 1937. Part of the former park survives as Curtiss Gardens together with its gate piers.

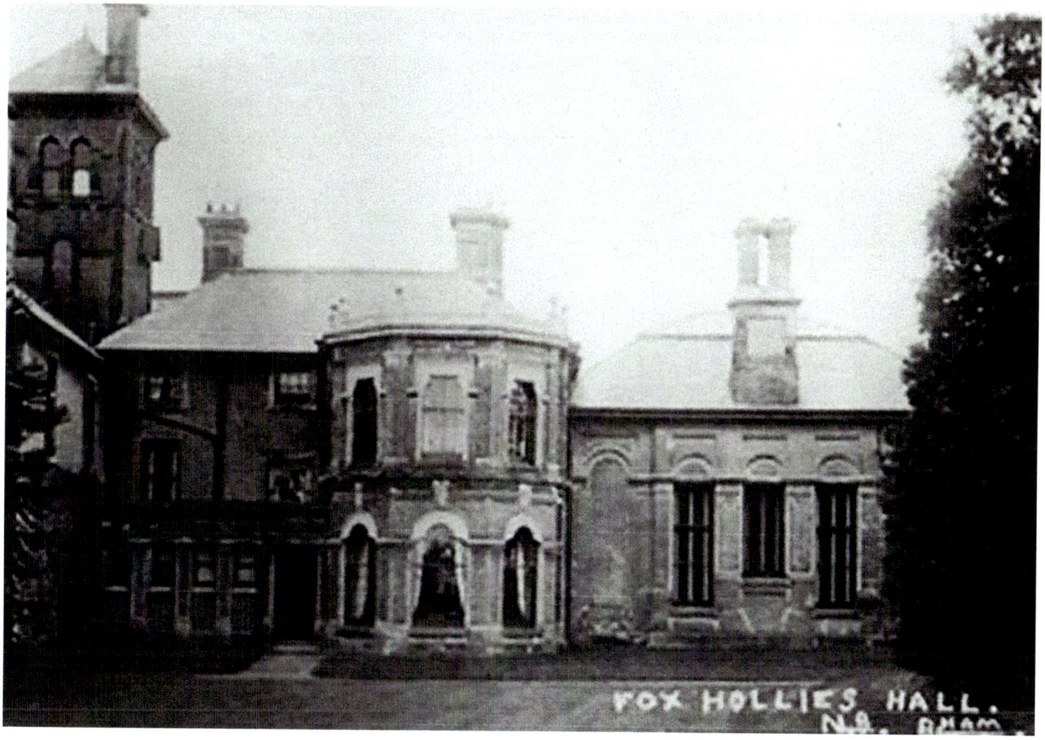

Fox Hollies' garden front, from a postcard. (James Darwin)

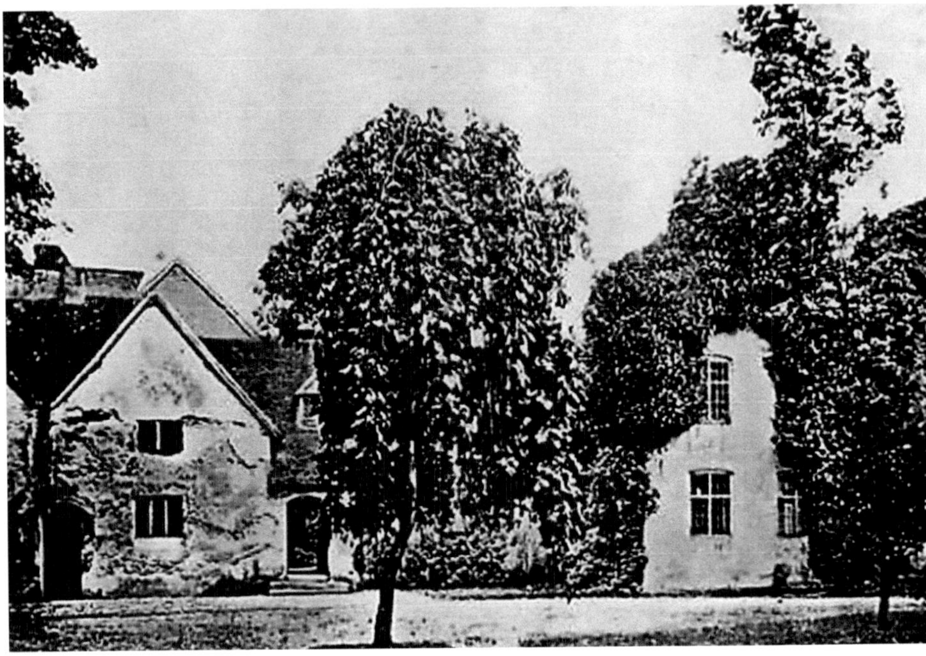

A nineteenth-century view of Hawne House as a farm. (Nicholas Kingsley)

54. Hawne House, Halesowen, Worcestershire. 1939

This was a substantial multiphase house of probably sixteenth-century origins, but with rambling late seventeenth- and further eighteenth-century additions. The estate was purchased by the banker and iron founder George Attwood (1722–1807) in 1748, being succeeded by his son, the banker Matthias DL JP MP (1746–1836). His son, the reforming MP Thomas Attwood (1783–1856), was born there but the house's principal nineteenth-century occupier was his younger sister Mary Anne, who died there aged ninety in 1872. The Attwood family sold it to a mining company in 1872, the house being thereafter tenanted as Hawne Farm. From the 1830s coal mining began to encroach and by the 1870s its setting was heavily compromised and in 1939 the house, by then derelict, was cleared away and the site redeveloped.

55. Bescot Hall, Walsall, Staffordshire. 1939

William Hillary held Bescot Hall around 1311 and by 1345 the family had received a licence to crenellate, the hall being duly fortified with a battlemented curtain wall with arrow slits. There was also a rectangular dry moat that was double-ditched on its north-western side and, before the end of the century, a chapel had been added. Sir Roger Hillary died in 1403, his heiress bringing it to William Mountfort of Coleshill in 1411, a descendant of Simon de Montfort, Earl of Leicester. On 30 January 1469, William's grandson, Sir Simon, was executed for treason but the forfeited estate was restored in 1534 to Thomas Mountford. By 1605 the Mountforts were recusants, the estate was compounded in 1648 and in 1678 the family's priest, Francis Dormer, was executed at Worcester. The house

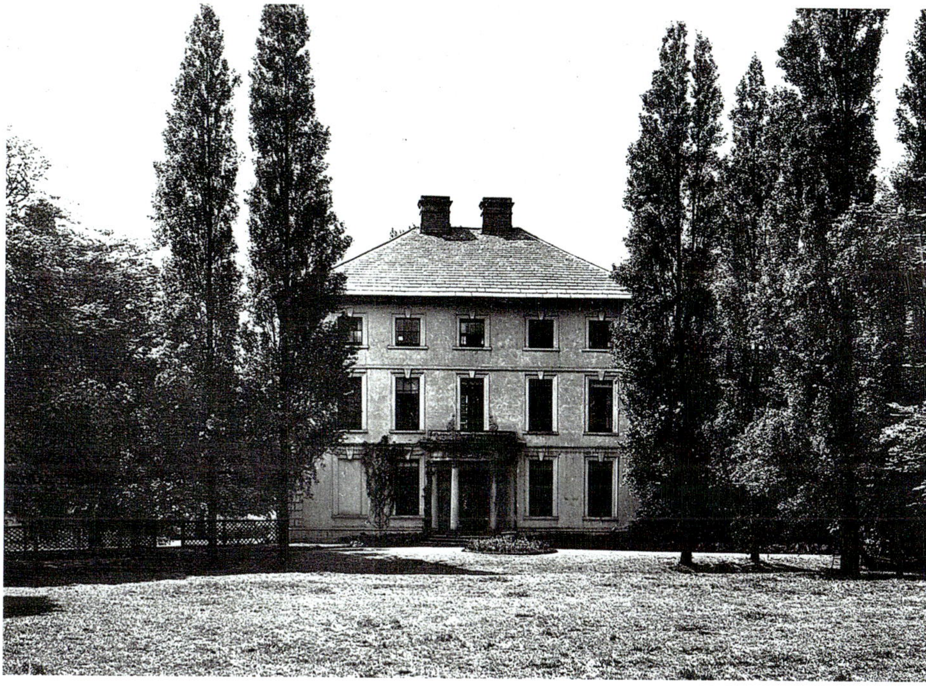

Bescot Hall in the 1900s, from a postcard. (J. Darwin)

had a few years before being assessed for tax on fourteen hearths. The last of the line, Edward, died in 1691, when it passed to his heiress's second husband, Jonas Slaney (d. 1717), whose son built a new two-storey, five-bay brick house with quoins and plat bands and a high hipped roof in 1727. In 1791 it was sold to the tenant, Richard Wilkes, with 80 acres for £3,200, but in 1794 was acquired by Richmond Aston of Tipton (d. 1796) for £4,000, who added a third storey and a semicircular Tuscan porch. His widow later enlarged the service wing and added a new drawing room. The estate was sold in 1820 to Edward, Stephen and John Crowther but by 1843 John was the sole owner, who left it in 1852 to his kinsman William Crowther (d. 1865), who let it, his trustees selling in 1872 to James Slater JP of Darlaston (d. 1901). Surviving photographs suggest that the interior had been at least partially remodelled in the later nineteenth century. Slater's widow died in April 1922, and the estate was sold to Pitt Bonarjee, a Congregational minister, who opened it as a private school, which failed in 1929. After several short lets, the land was sold and it became derelict. The bridge over the moat was lost in 1937 and the house demolished in 1939.

56. Tennal Hall, Harborne, Warwickshire. *c.* 1940

Tennal was a substantial, if rambling, timber-framed mansion with a sixteenth-century hall and close studded cross wing. It was enlarged in the century following and long the seat of the Milwards, a cadet branch of the Milwards of Alvechurch. Its rear elevation was partly refaced in brick and given large, mullioned windows in the later nineteenth century, but its original close studding survived on its side

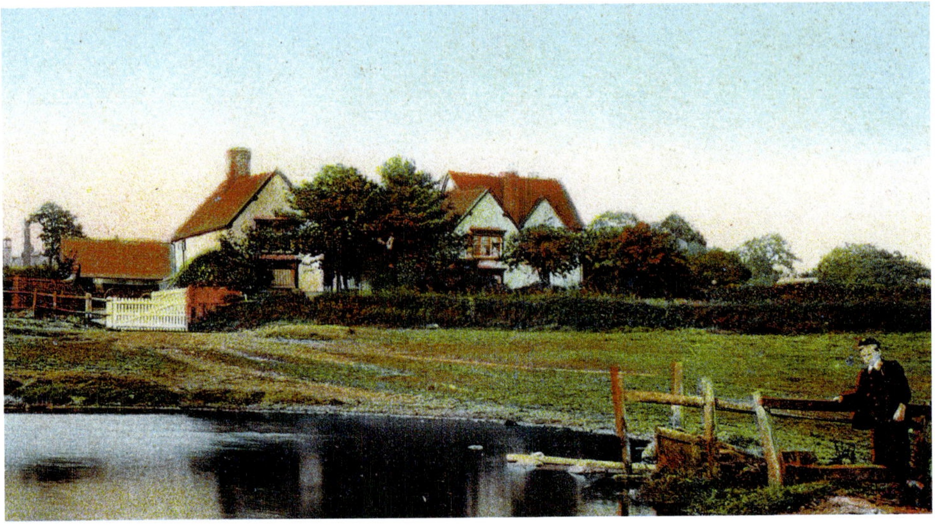

Tennal Hall from the fields, *c.* 1906, from a postcard. (J. Darwin)

and entrance elevations. At its rear was an extensive courtyard of agricultural buildings. There is a nineteenth-century oil painting of the house in the collection of Birmingham Museum Trust. By the end of the nineteenth century its setting was becoming rapidly suburbanised. Its land housed a golf club between 1910 and 1935, and the reminder of the estate was purchased for a housing development in 1939 and the house demolished a year later.

57. Showell Green House, Sparkhill, Warwickshire. 1940

The merchant and Unitarian William Russell (1740–1818) bought an estate at Showell Green, which included an early eighteenth-century two-storey brick farmhouse, to which he added a three-storey extension with a canted bay. This was burnt out on 16 July 1791 during the latter stages of the destructive Church and King riot. The Russells followed the similarly afflicted Priestley to the US in 1794. The house was repaired but later replaced by a stuccoed early nineteenth-century villa of two storeys and asymmetrical canted bays, seat of banker James Lloyd in the mid-nineteenth century. His family sold a large portion of the estate separately for building in 1853. The villa was later the home of Joseph Stock, but in 1910 the house became the John Taylor Memorial Home, rented from the nearby Women's Hospital. It was damaged by a bomb in 1940 and later demolished to allow for the expansion of the Women's Hospital.

58. Moundsley Hall, Kings Norton, Worcestershire. 1940

Moundsley was a mid-nineteenth-century gabled neo-Tudor house which was built for Thomas Lane, who had purchased the estate in 1843 from Edward Dawson. It, however, contained within its fabric substantial remains of an early sixteenth-century gabled timber-framed structure which had been the home of the Field family until around 1770. Lane was succeeded by his son Charles Pelham Lane JP, who died in 1936. The estate was then sold to Birmingham Corporation,

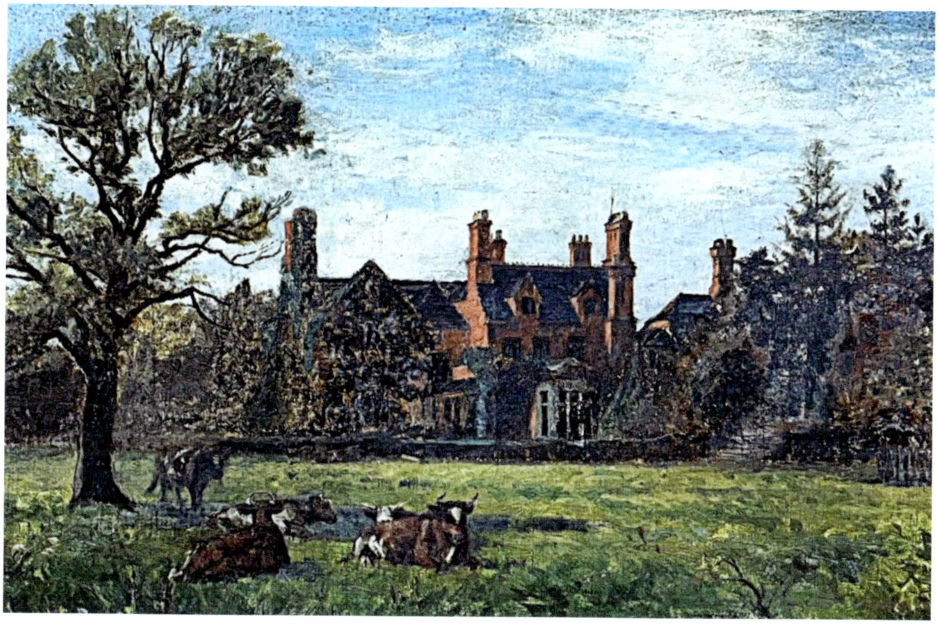

Moundsley Hall, oil painting by W. B. Fortescue, *c.* 1891. (Gardiner Houlgate Ltd)

but the house demolished in 1940. Fortunately, the earlier timber-framed structure was recorded and a report on the building appeared in the 1947 Birmingham Archaeological Society journal. Its stables and lodge houses remain Grade II listed.

59. Ward End Hall, Ward End, Warwickshire. *c.* 1945

Ward End originally supported a sizable moated manor house, seat of the eponymous Wards, who sold to John Bond *c.* 1512, who enclosed a 30-acre park. It subsequently passed from the Bonds to the Kynnersleys and then the Baylys. After the Civil War the house was completely dismantled. The site was acquired by ironmaster Charles Blackham, who in 1710 built a new house in brick with stone dressings just to the west of the moat, the three-storey classical house consisting of the central block only, with four room to each floor and a central wide entrance hall leading to a fine timber staircase behind. The estate was sold to Abraham Spooner in 1749, although when the heir, Abraham Spooner Lillingston, was accidently killed by a falling tree at Elmdon (q.v.) in 1834, Ward End was sold to the Huttons. Samuel Hutton (d. 1848) seems to have made immediate alterations, although his successor William Hutton also rebuilt the house, the additions designed by J. J. Bateman in the late 1850s. Surviving correspondence suggests that William Hutton was a difficult and quarrelsome client (like his forebear at Red House (q.v.)), although whether the architect and builder had done anything to deserve his vitriol and late payments is debatable. Bateman's alterations were remarkably conservative and they included adding the flanking wings, which contained new drawing and dining rooms, and remodelling the principal façade to produce a one closely resembling that of Charlemont (q.v.) of a decade before. The two flanking wings were single storey with a high parapet (that on the east

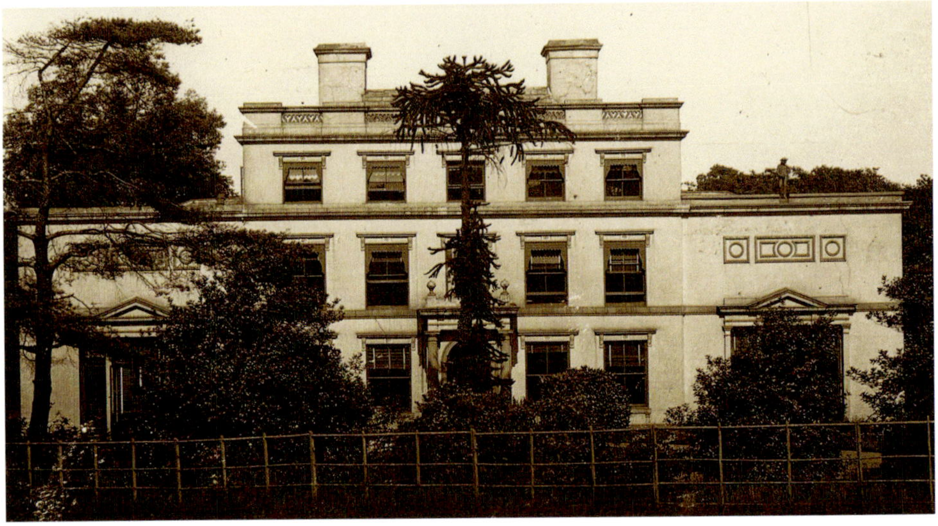

Ward End Hall, *c.* 1908, from a postcard. (James Darwin)

side supporting a lead figural statue) hiding a hipped roof, embellished with a geometric frieze. Bateman also added a classical porch and rendered the lot. The house's contents were sold by William Hutton in October 1884. A large winter garden was added by his successor to the south-west wing during the 1880s. By the outbreak of the Second World War the house stood derelict and after the war ended it was cleared for council housing.

60. Priory (The), Kings Heath, Warwickshire. *c.* 1947

This was a substantial early nineteenth-century, crenellated, stuccoed mansion in mild Gothic with crenellated parapet and an attached crenellated stable block, gates and brick park wall. It was originally known as Bleak House and stood close to Kings Heath House on Vicarage Road. It was built by James Anderton but was purchased by James Cartland in 1845 and the house altered for his son around 1855 using J. J. Bateman, who also extended the Cartlands' works in St Mary's Square around the same time. The house was again altered in 1864–67 and renamed 'The Priory', again to the designs of Bateman, the builder being William Matthews. An elaborate full-height neo-Tudor canted bay window was added to the garden elevation, lighting the dining room, and the former billiard room, above which it also lit, was remodelled to form a drawing room. Also remodelled was the stable yard, much of the stabling being replaced, complete with iron fittings by Musgraves of Belfast and Minton tiles, and a lodge was also built. A large conservatory, which housed a collection of exotic tropical caged birds, appears to have been added around the same time. The Priory Trust Co. Ltd, founded by Cartland in 1880, began buying neighbouring property for the purpose of development. The contents of the house were sold by auction in August 1940 after the death of Major J. H. Cartland, but the house then stood empty and by 1947, when it was demolished, it was in poor repair. A school now occupies the site but the now Grade II listed lodge house survives.

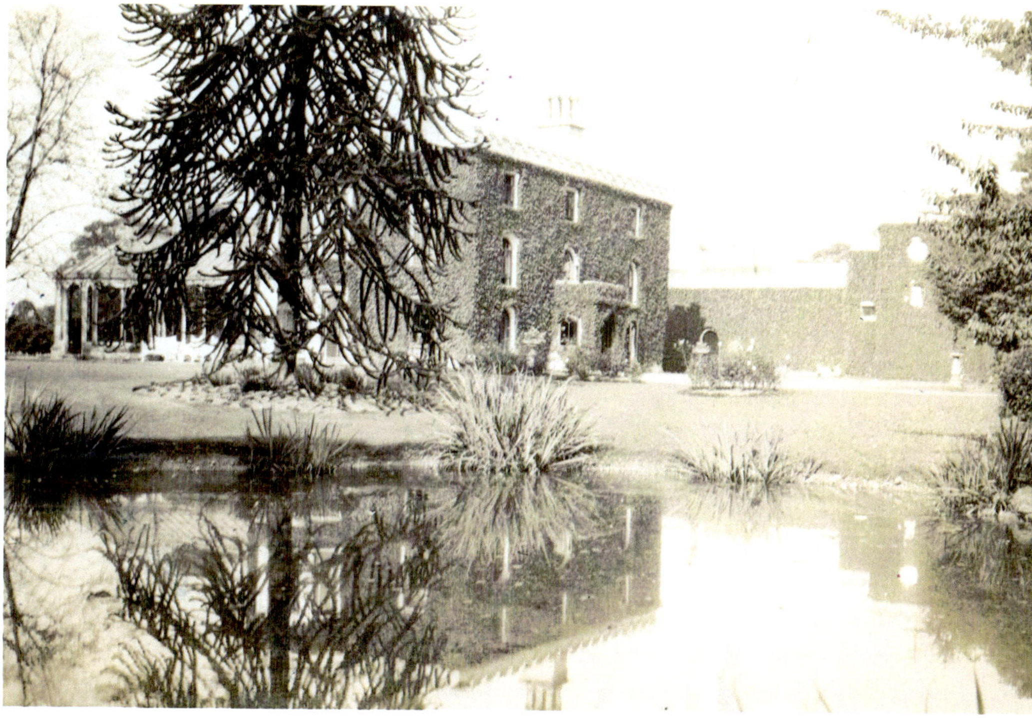

The Priory seen from the lake, *c*. 1897. (James Cartland)

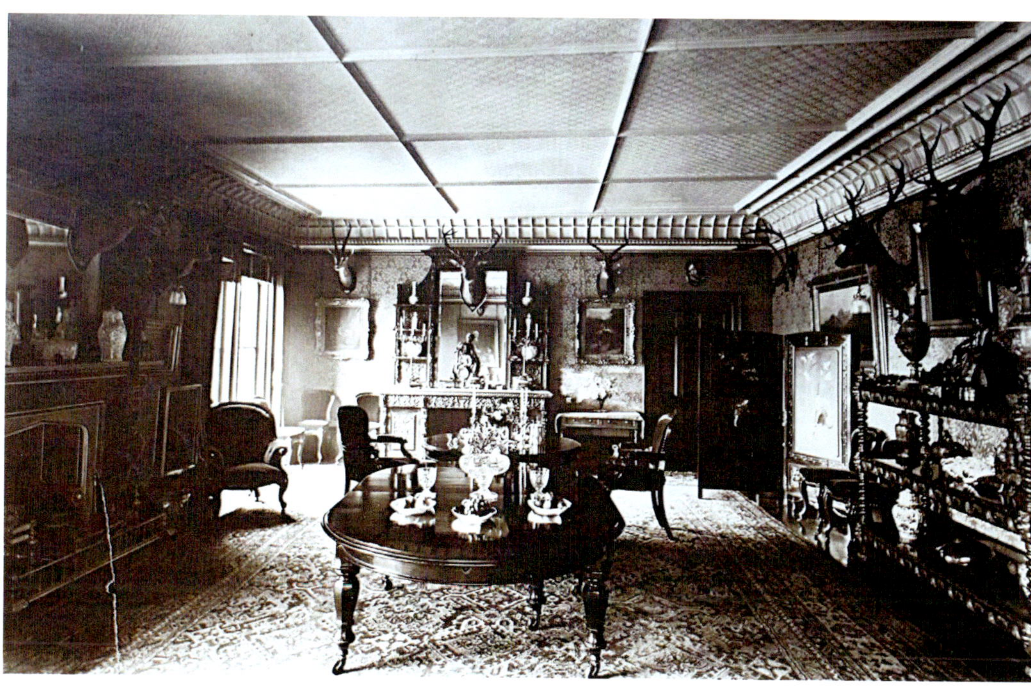

The Priory's dining room, *c*. 1897. (James Cartland)

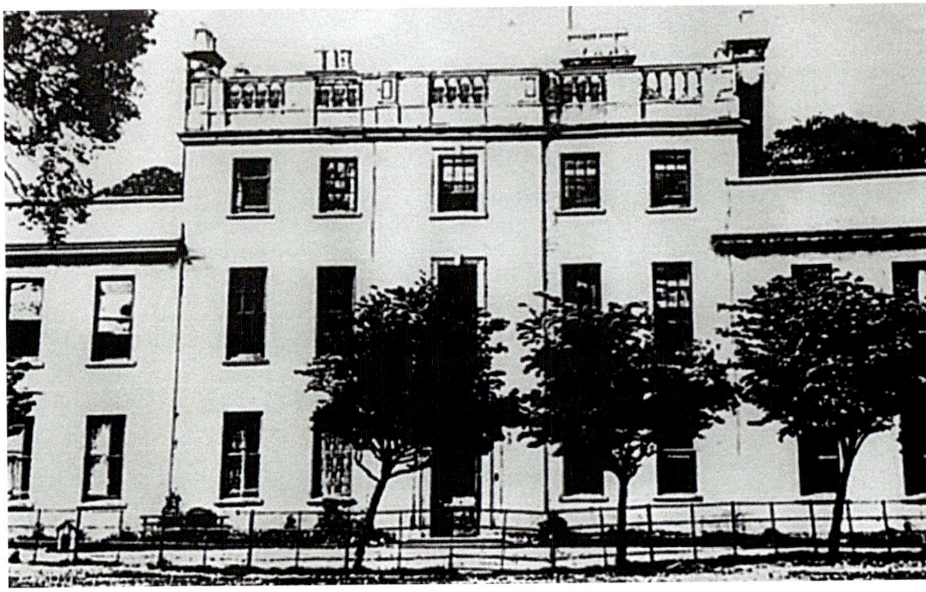

Charlemont entrance front, *c.* 1906. (James Darwin)

61. Charlemont Hall, West Bromwich, Staffordshire. 1948

Charlemont was a three-by-three bay, two-and-a-half-storey villa with a hipped roof that was built in 1755 for Jesson Lowe to replace an earlier mid-seventeenth-century house called Crump Hall, which had been destroyed by fire. The last of the Lowes died in 1793 and the estate was inherited by Dr John Hallam, Dean of Bristol. In 1804 the grounds were improved by diverting a nearby highway for the dean's son. The estate was let to Thomas Jesson in 1813 but the freehold was sold with part of the estate to Samuel J. Dawes in 1825. He later expanded the grounds by acquiring further adjoining land from Henry Hallam, altering the house to the designs of Charles Edge in 1843–44, who probably added the lower wings, resulting in a house which resembled (and was perhaps the inspiration for) Ward End Hall (q.v.). The east wing was added in 1855 for Colonel John Nock Bagnall, an ironmaster who had purchased the house the previous year, but it was let from around 1871. Its last occupier was Thomas Jones, town clerk of Wednesbury, and the house was demolished in 1948.

62. Elmdon Hall, Solihull, Warwickshire. 1948

Elmdon was begun by Abraham Spooner, ironmaster, in 1785 to replace an earlier house that had been the seat of the Botelers, the Hores and the Maynes. The house had a seven-bay, two-and-a-half storey entrance front with Tuscan pilasters supporting a pediment, a similar garden front and with one side elevation that had a central full-height bow giving views out over the lake. The entrance hall had a columned screen of Siena marble, the bow-windowed library boasted fine mahogany bookcases and there was a 31 feet by 21 feet drawing room with a fine marble chimneypiece. The architect was perhaps John Standbridge working in classical mode, who had been commissioned by Spooner to rebuild the parish

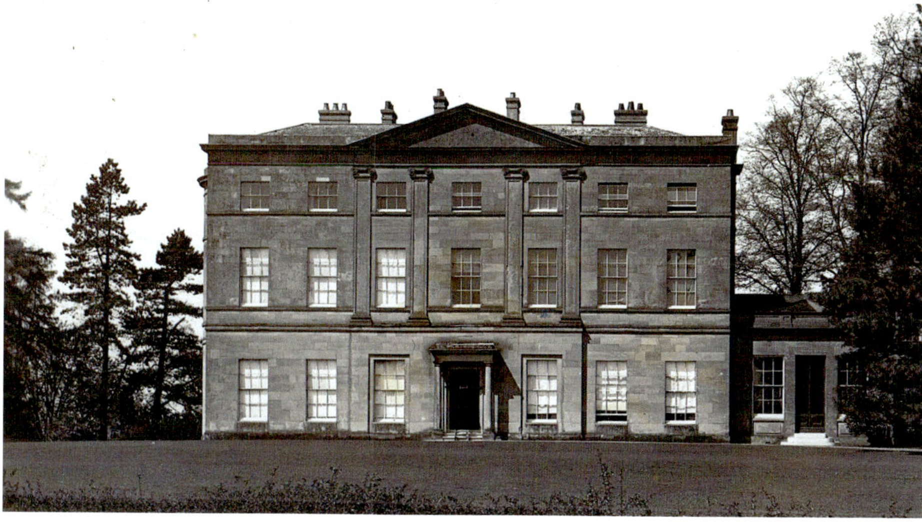

Elmdon Hall, from a postcard of *c.* 1906. (James Darwin)

church and the façade closely resembles that of Whateley Hall (q.v.). The house was completed after his death by his son, Revd Isaac Spooner. Its contents were sold in 1834, Isaac's son, Abraham Spooner Lillingston, having been killed by a falling tree in the park. In 1835 the house was let, but the estate was sold to William Charles Alston in 1840. His homonymous son altered and extended the house in 1864. The contents were sold in 1920 along with outlying portions of the estate. The remaining portions of the estate including the hall were sold in 1930. By 1936 proposals were put forward to develop the park, but in 1939 the house was described as derelict. Despite claims that the house was occupied by the Home Guard during the Second World War it seems in fact to have already been too decayed to be considered suitable to serve any purpose. It was demolished by Solihull Council in 1948 when described as little more than a shell. In 1950 the church was described as standing within the park of the 'now vanished' hall. Part of its parkland are now a public park. A fine classical lodge house survives.

63. Darlaston Hall, Willenhall, Staffordshire. *c.* 1950

William de Darlaston was established here in 1255 and his posterity flourished until the family ended in heiresses in 1418, after which the estate passed to Roger Wilkes in 1432 and then to Edward Hayes, followed by the Lords Stafford and in 1555 Edward, 1st Lord North from whom it came to John Crewe of Crewe in Cheshire, whose family still held the estate in 1810. Stebbing Shaw makes no mention of a house here in his time, but early in the nineteenth century a substantial three-storey house was erected, seven bays by four, lit at the main front by tripartite sashes, all centered by a stone Doric portico and topped by hipped roofs. In 1870 what is now Cothill School had been established in the grounds but this moved to Oxfordshire in 1879 and it was acquired by Richard Mills JP, who remained there for two decades. The house was in poor repair when photographed

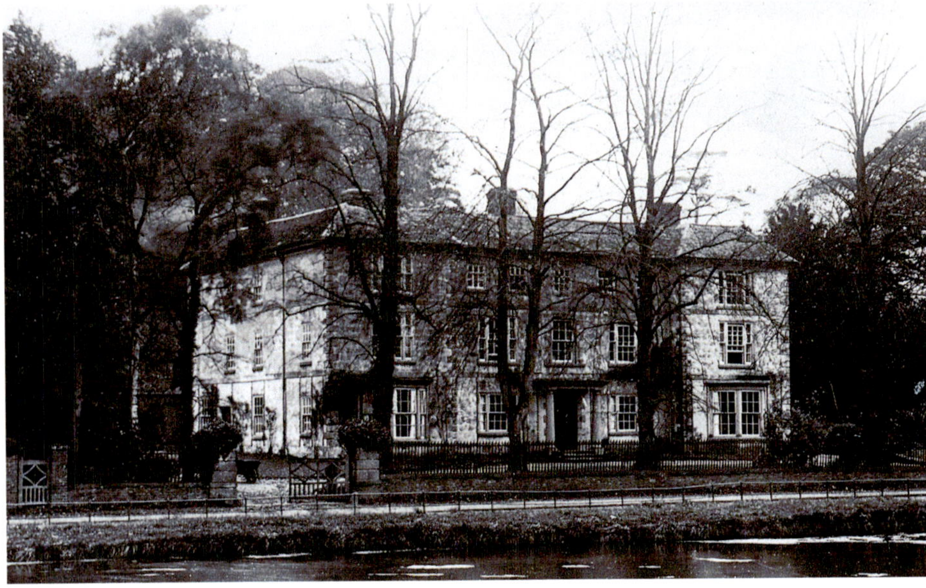

Darlaston Hall's entrance front in 1907, from a postcard. (James Darwin)

by the National Monuments Record in 1942 and it was demolished in about 1950, its continued use compromised by the intense industrialisation of the area.

64. Perry Pont House, Perry Barr, Staffordshire. 1951

Perry Pont began life as a relatively standard three-bay, two-storey stuccoed late Regency villa standing in extensive grounds bounded by the River Tame on two sides, but which soon afterwards acquired a substantial two-storey wing attached

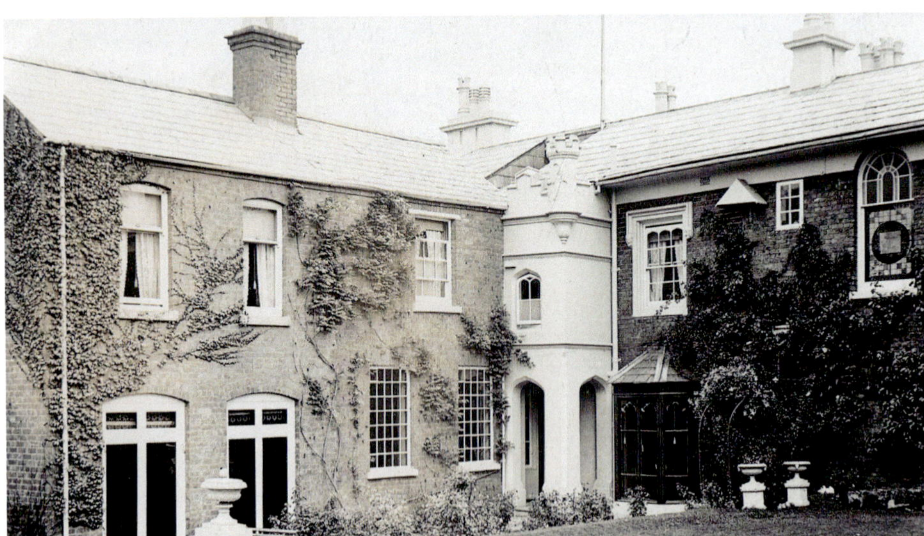

Perry Pont's rear elevation showing the later wing and Gothic tower. (James Darwin)

to the rear of the main house with a small Gothic turret complete with miniature bartizan. The builder was wine merchant and coal dealer William Henry Osborn, who also laid out impressive gardens before 1838 – 'one of the most perfect little paradises which any man could desire' – through which were scattered grottoes, statues and follies, including a miniature church, complete with a font and altar, which could contain six people. One folly had an arched entrance and stained-glass windows, with oyster shells set into the roof; another had a miniature of Cleopatra's Needle at the entrance and inside a mosaic floor made of horse's teeth and animal bones; its stained glass was filled with imagery of unicorns and lions. At the turn of the century the house was home to Thomas Jenkins and family, who were there until at least the First World War, but by 1938 it was empty and reported as under threat of demolition. Its fate was delayed by the war, but in 1951 it was cleared away and the site became a builder's yard.

65. Willenhall House, Binley, Warwickshire. 1952

This house was built in 1831 on a 4-acre site by William, 2nd Earl of Craven, for agent, Mr Wyatt, of his Coombe Abbey estate on which it stood. Under Wyatt's direction, the estate foreman and his team eclectically adapted an eighteenth-century brick farmhouse to create a stuccoed late Regency villa of asymmetrical appearance and eccentric outline. The arched portico was enclosed by a pair of chimneybreasts disguised as antae and two fronts were endowed with full-height canted bays. It was a large stuccoed classical villa with a high parapet. After Wyatt's time, it was let to Maj. Gen. William Battine CBN (1785–1852), formerly

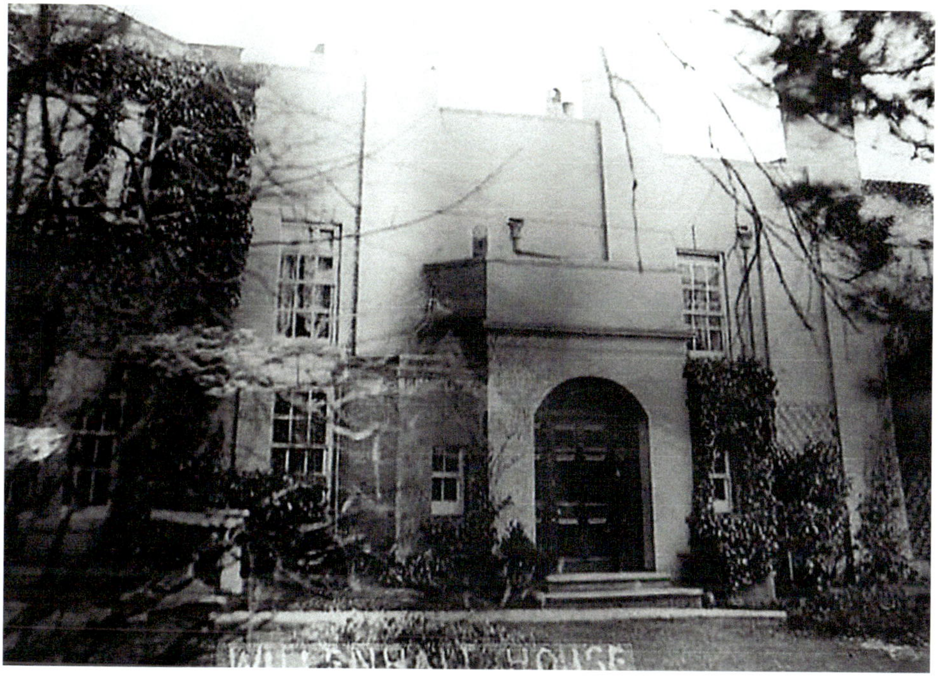

Willenhall House at the turn of the century, from a postcard. (Private collection)

of the Bengal Army. The house was sold in 1923 along with much of the rest of the Combe Abbey estate, but eventually came into the ownership of Coventry City Council. During the Second World War the house was used for fire training, which left it in a poor state, following which, finding no viable use, it fell into dereliction and was demolished in 1952.

66. Whitley Abbey, Coventry, Warwickshire. 1953

The Whitley estate came to Bartholomew Tate MP (d. 1601) from the Longvilles and he or his son, Sir William (d. 1618), built a new house here, Whitley Hall. It was Jacobean with a central great hall range sandwiched between two cross wings, all topped with gables. After his death Zouch Tate sold the estate to John Bowater in 1627 from whose family it passed to the Whelers and their daughter and heiress in 1774 brought it to Henry, later 2nd Viscount Hood (d. 1836). The house was extended by the office of Sir John Soane in 1807–10 and the house name was changed to Whitley Abbey, but these severely classical designs seem not to have ben proceeded with and the changes were, in the end, done in Jacobean style, but it is possible that one of Soane's assistant went solo and undertook the work – the enlarged hall, at least, was Soanian. It was sold by the 4th Viscount in 1867 to E. H. Petre of a notable recusant family. In his time, a fire in 1874 led to an extensive rebuild including the addition of a chapel. Drawings by J. G. Crace for redecoration of the interior of *c.* 1888 survive. In 1920, the son, O. H. P. Turville-Petre, sold up, the house having been used previously to lodge Belgian refugees. By the mid-1930s the area had begun to be suburbanised and it was purchased by Coventry Corporation. It lingered on in several, largely temporary, uses until cleared for the building of a school in 1953.

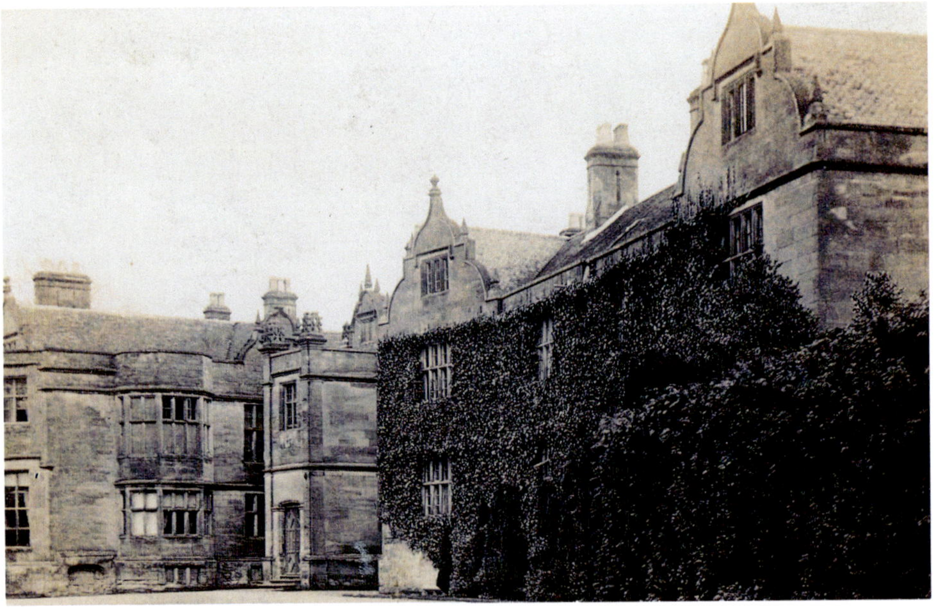

Whitley Abbey from a postcard, *c.* 1904. (James Darwin)

67. Pendeford Hall, Tettenhall, Staffordshire. 1953

The estate of 950 acres came to James Fowler from Rowland Lee, Bishop of Coventry, after the Dissolution of the Monasteries, Pendeford Hall being built to replace a Tudor predecessor in 1670 (dated over the entrance), by Walter Fowler III in Artisan Mannerist style, two piles deep with a five-bay, two-storey façade and topped by a trio of curly shaped gables with attic mullioned windows and quadruple clustered stacks rising behind. There was a plat band above the ground floor supporting the segmental pediment of the entrance and the end bays

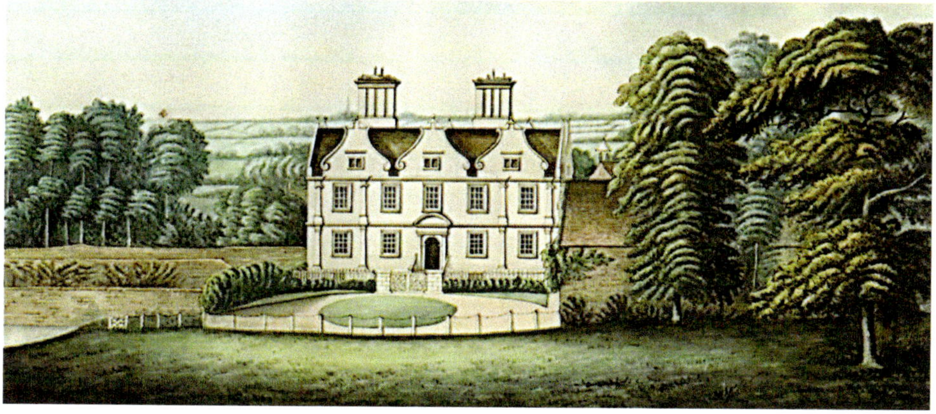

Pendeford Hall in the late eighteenth century after J. R. Ferneyhough. (Public domain)

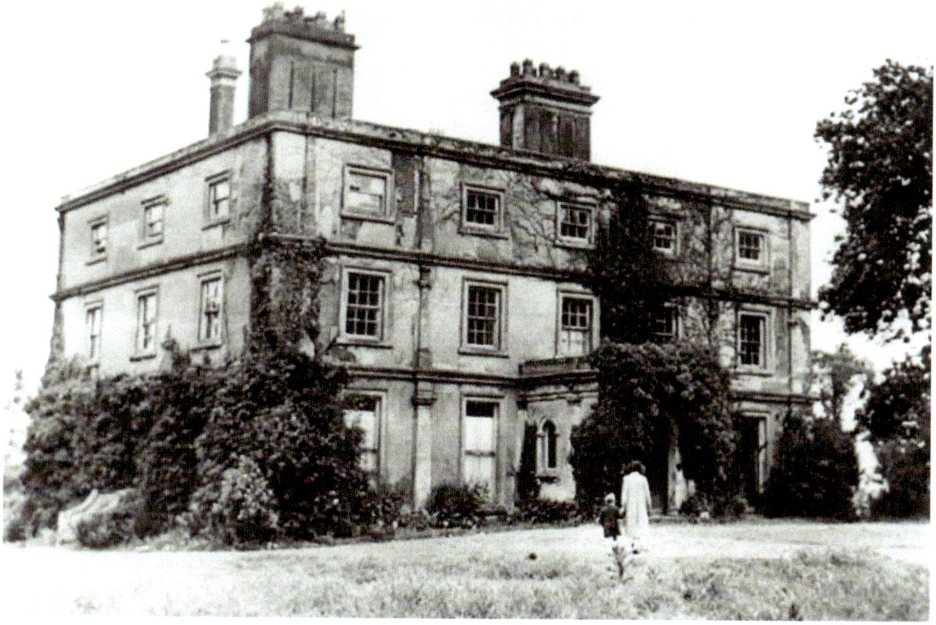

Pendeford Hall in terminal decay, *c.* 1951. (Private collection)

were enclosed by pilasters, Ionic over Doric, supporting a thin entablature. The attic gables seem to owe something to a group of Yorkshire houses like Hellaby, Grimethorpe and Norton Conyers. T. F. Pritchard of Shrewsbury supplied a chimneypiece and made alterations, Stebbing Shaw writing that in 1795 it had 'a very picturesque appearance, being a square uniform fabric of stone, light and handsome' with rooms that were 'plain and good'. He added that in 1796 the roof was raised, eliding the gables, providing a full attic storey, extending the pilasters, replacing the roof and adding a substantial portico, all to no good effect. It was let in 1815 to Richard Evans (1769–1841), coach proprietor of the Red Lion, Wolverhampton. When his younger son John died in 1864 it reverted to Richard Fowler-Butler, who let it at first, but the family was still in residence in 1936. After the Second World War it lay derelict and was demolished in 1953 to be replaced by housing.

68. Falcon Lodge, Sutton Coldfield, Warwickshire. 1954

The house was originally a three-bay, two-and-a-half-storey, mid-eighteenth-century brick farmhouse belonging to the Pepper family, standing in 54 acres. In 1828–29 it was extended by a wide full-height canted bay at one end and given a ground-floor bow at the other, all being unified by a coat of Roman cement and embellished at roof level with an embattled parapet for Nottingham industrialist

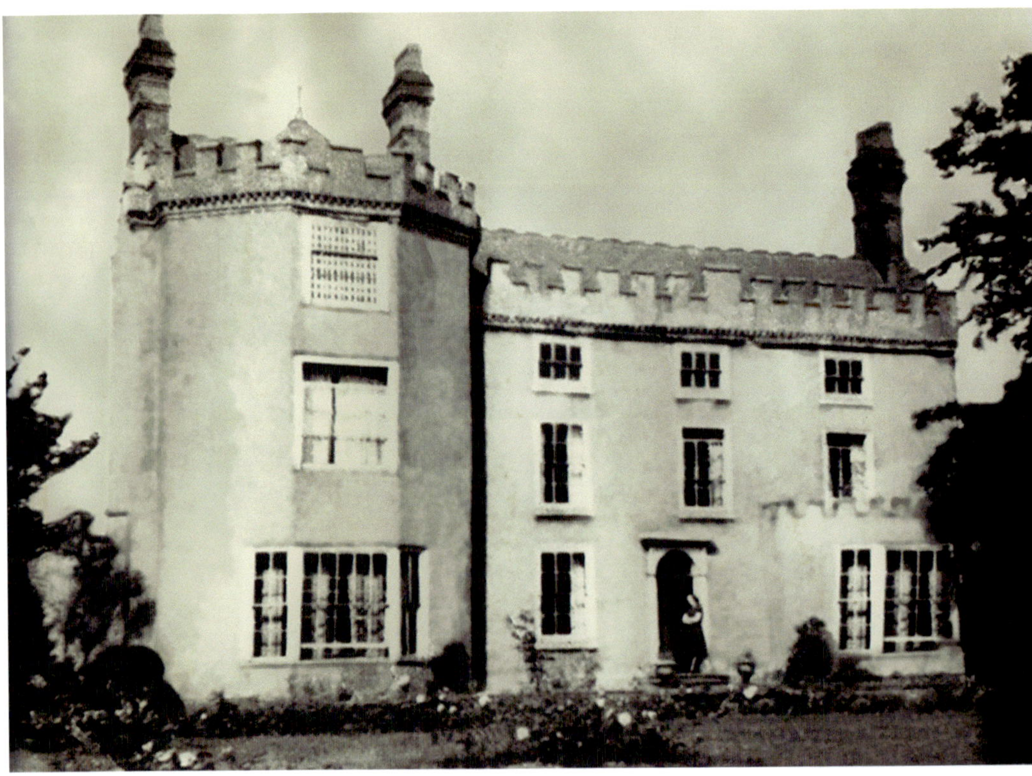

Falcon Lodge, photographed *c.* 1950 with Annie Smith in the doorway. (CC BY-SA 4.0)

William Pepper, the architect being G. Elliott, a local surveyor with the builder Solomon Smith of Four Oaks. A considerable amount of internal reordering also took place. It remined the home of William Pepper until his death in 1862, when it was sold to absentee Maj. Thomas Terry, the 1862 sales particulars describing the house as being 'adapted for a family of the first respectability'. It was then let to Francis Parkes, who farmed 120 acres in 1871. The house and part of the estate were purchased by a local chemist, Cattell, as an investment in 1919 and he sold much of it to Sutton Council in 1937 for £37,500, with the remainder of the land being acquired in 1947, with municipal housing being built on the estate from 1948 to 1956. The Smith family were the last tenants, leaving *c.* 1951, and the house went three years later.

69. Wassell Grove, Stourbridge, Worcestershire. *c.* 1954

A late seventeenth-century brick house of five bays and two storeys beneath a high hipped roof with at least one cross wing and an entrance under a curved hood, Wassell was long the seat of the Rogers, glassmakers. It was sold on the death of banker Daniel Rogers (qv Hill House, Amblecote) in 1829 and acquired by John Richards MP and greatly enlarged to the designs of Charles Edge in 1831–33, adding stables and a lodge. Survey drawings of 1829 show a plain two-storey, five-bay, eighteenth-century brick main block to which Edge added a coat of stucco, a pediment and pilasters. To the east return two full-height bows were added but whilst the terrace level ground-floor windows were part of the build, the Doric portico (hiding an arched entrance) was a later addition. Further minor alterations were undertaken in the mid-nineteenth century by Thomas Naden.

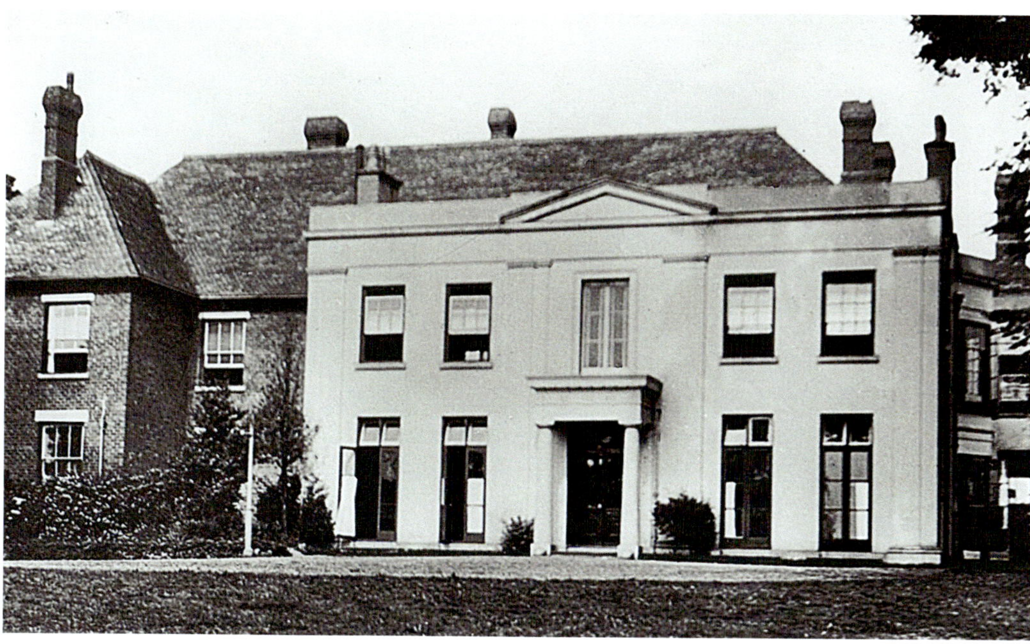

Wassell Grove in its days as a convalescent home from a 1931 postcard. (M. Craven)

It was later home of Job Garrett JP in the later nineteenth century. During the First World War it became a convalescent home but was later considerably extended for use as a hospital. The coming of the NHS led to its replacement elsewhere and it was all demolished in 1954. It's now residentially converted stables, lodge, dovecote and garden walls survive.

70. Pedmore Hall, Stourbridge, Worcestershire. 1955

The original house was built by Robert Arderne and dated from 1607, but it was rebuilt by Thomas Foley (d. 1671) from 1668. It was later the home of Arthur Annesley, 8th Viscount Valentia from the 1770s until his elevation as 1st Earl of Mountnorris in 1793. Later the seat of Richard Homer by the 1830s, he died there in 1847, being succeeded by Revd Keeling Freeman. Latterly it was a distinguished three-storey neoclassical house with a rendered five-bay façade divided by Doric pilasters over a rustic containing the entrance. The Palladian tradition was also continued in a pair of two-storey projections with lower hipped roof to the entrance front. The house evidently contained the remains of a much earlier building, as within was a fine 1670 geometric staircase and high-quality early eighteenth-century wainscot. One of the side wings was latterly partly roofless and appears to have undergone some considerable modification in the later nineteenth century. It was demolished in 1955 and replaced by a modern house, built around the remaining stable block, which acquired an overscale giant tetrastyle attached pedimented portico in 2010; the seventeenth-century staircase survives within.

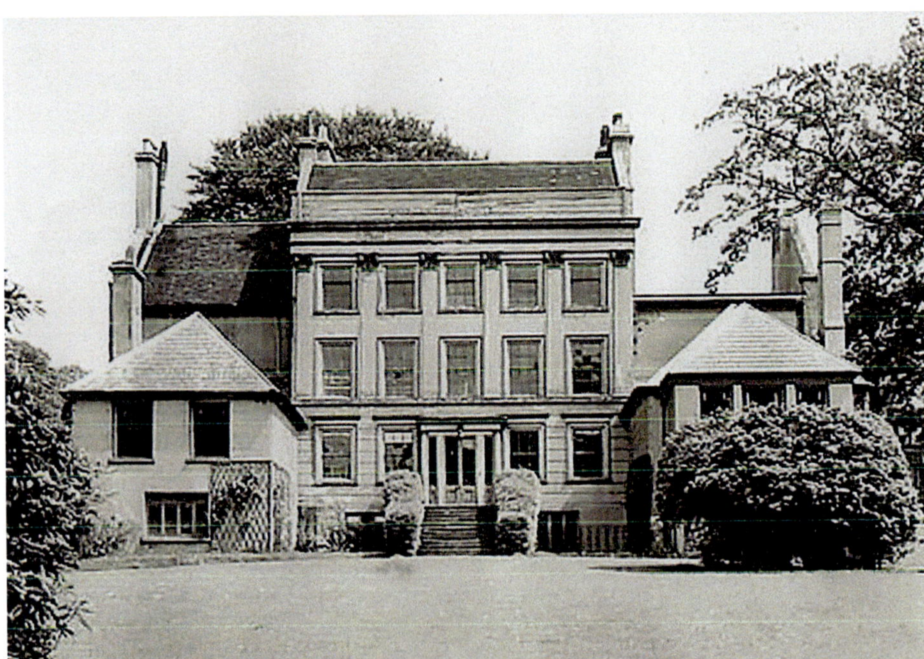

Pedmore Hall's garden front in 1955. (National Monuments Record)

71. Oakwood House, West Bromwich, Staffordshire. 1955

The estate was held by the Turtons of Alrewas, whose seat was The Oaks or Oak House, which is now preserved as a museum. A portion of the estate called Oakley's Croft was sold to Thomas Jesson of Sutton Coldfield (d. 1703) in 1679 and he built a late seventeenth-century brick manor house. The central part of the house was of brick and had a symmetrical two-storey front of five bays with a heavy wooden cornice supporting a shaped gable-ended roof with attic dormers. The house was extended on either side in the eighteenth century and had a small early nineteenth-century addition to its garden façade. Its fine mid-eighteenth-century staircase had three turned balusters per tread and a ramped handrail. In the mid nineteenth the estate consisted of 43 acres of land. It was let by Thomas Jesson to William Bagnall in the mid-nineteenth century, but Jesson returned and died there in 1873, being succeeded by his son, a parson, who presented it to the people of West Bromwich in 1912, the local authority ultimately expressing their gratitude by neglecting and, in 1955, demolishing it, although the grounds remain a public park.

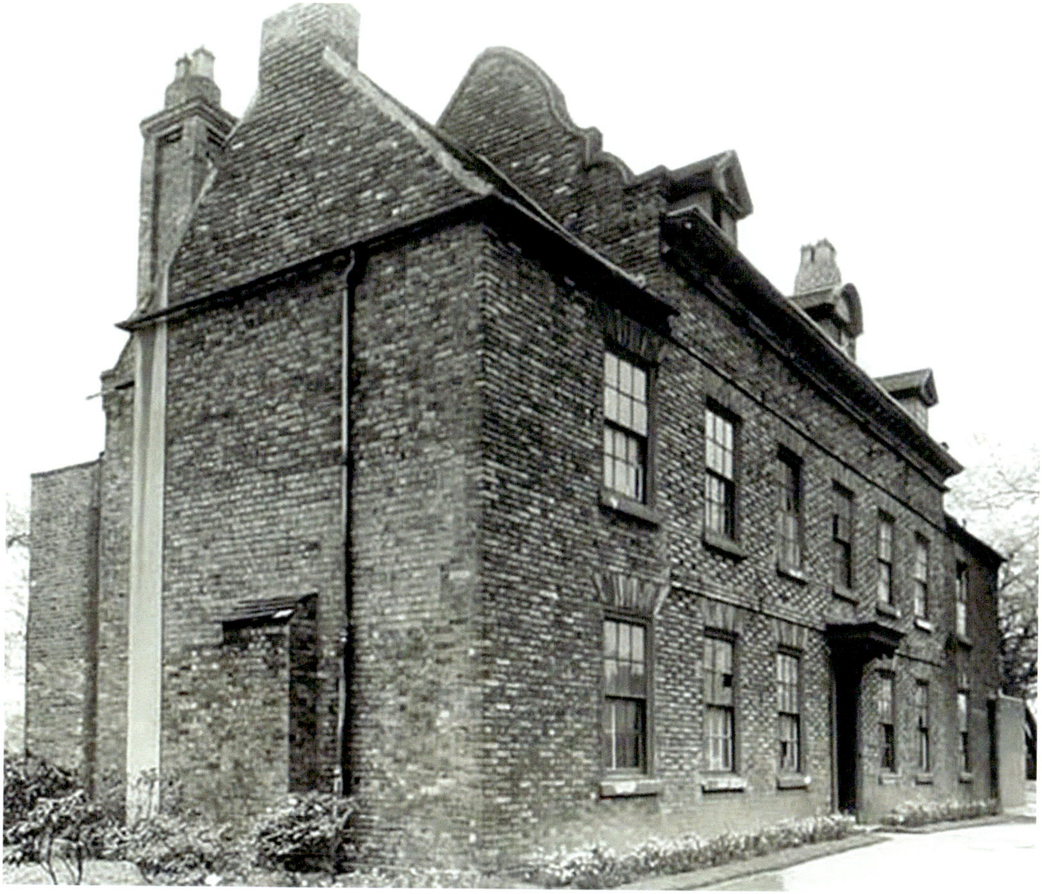

Oakwood House's entrance front, *c.* 1956. (National Monuments Record)

72. Hawkesley Hall, Longbridge, Warwickshire. 1956

There had been a medieval manor house here within a moat, seat of Richard de Haweslow in 1280 and in 1424 John Haweslow granted some of his lands there (the name Hawkesley is late) to Humphrey Stafford. William Middlemore bought the estate in 1549 and the family held the estate until the Restoration. The original timber-framed manor house was demolished in 1850. Its successor, on a nearby site, appears to date from the mid-eighteenth century with shaped gable on two fronts, as used on Ecton House (Northants) and attributed by the later Professor Gomme to William Hiorn, whose nearby Broome Hall is very similar; the cambered sashes are also in the Hiorn mould, but were dropped to terrace level in the Regency period when stucco and faux quoins were added. A Gothic porch and a rear range were provided in 1850 and there was a coach house of similar date with shaped gables which appear to have been attached to considerably earlier barns. Demolished for municipal housing, the site of hall itself is now part of a small park.

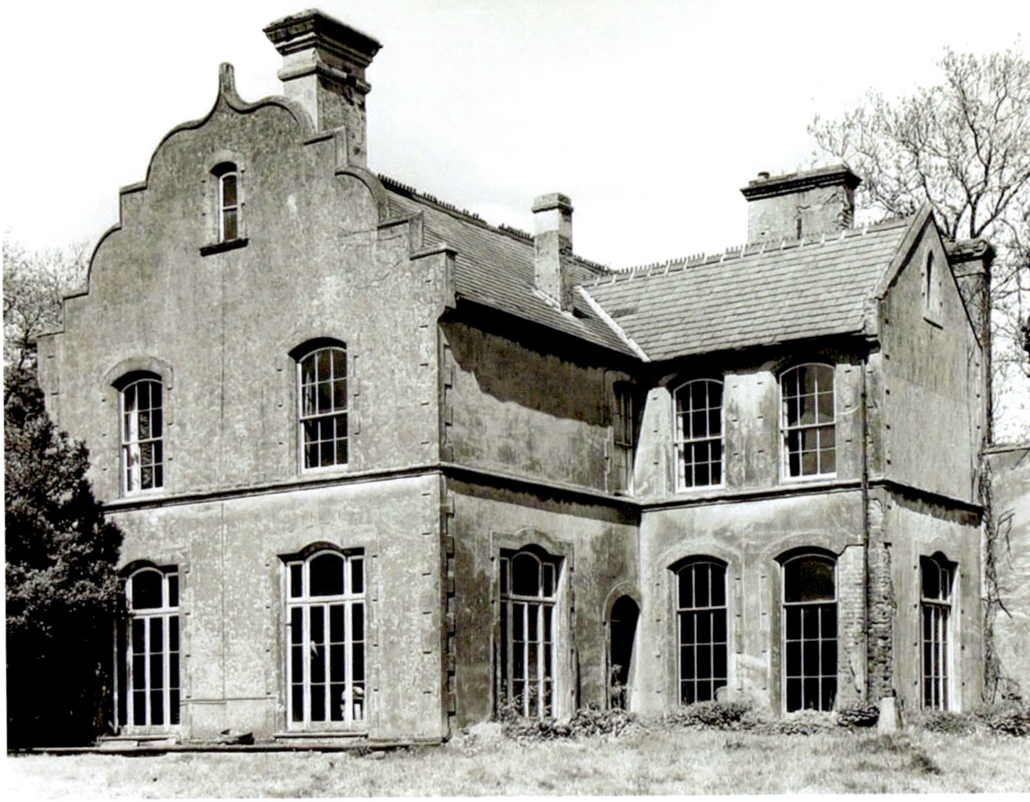

Hawkesley Hall's south front. (National Monuments Record)

73. Warley Abbey, Bearwood, Smethwick, Staffordshire. 1957

In 1792 Samuel Galton the younger of Great Barr Hall purchased an estate with a seventeenth-century house at Warley, from the Russell family. He called in Humphrey Repton in 1794 to landscape what had previously been an agricultural landscape and refront the house. In 1810 when his son Hubert Galton came of age, he went to live there, calling in Robert Lugar (1773–1855) to rebuild the house in Gothic style, 1819–20, with much crenellation, four centred arched fenestration, pinnacles and canted bays, all culminating in a porch like a pintle advancing from a tower with a pyramidal roof – all picturesquely bizarre. In the mid-nineteenth century, a billiard room wing and other reception rooms in the neo-Tudor style were added to the entrance front.

After Galton's death in 1864 the house went through several owners: H. G. Read MP in the 1880s, followed by glassmaker Alexander Macombe Chance, who engineered its purchase, partly by public subscription, by Birmingham Corporation in 1902. It was opened to the public as a Birmingham park (although not then in Birmingham) in 1906. Unfortunately, lack of both use and maintenance sealed the fate of the house, which was demolished in 1957. Repton's Doric Temple and Lugar's lodges have also gone. Its park is a Grade II registered landscape.

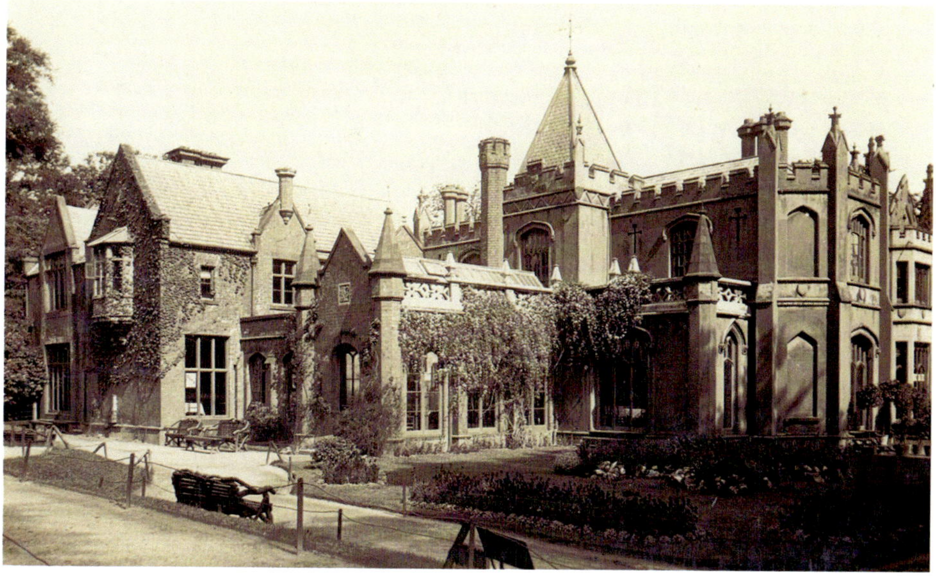

Warley Abbey, *c.* 1910, from a postcard. (James Darwin)

74. Netherby Hall, Sedgley, Staffordshire. 1959

The Haden family had been prominent in Sedgley and Dudley since at least the eighteenth century, and in the second quarter of the nineteenth century elected to build (or rebuild) as a villa, which they called Netherby. A two-storey, three-by-three-bay villa, it was tricked up in Gothic trappings and provided with a three-storey central bay rising like a clerestory and flanked by slim crenellated turrets. There were mullioned and transom windows and elaborate cresting. There

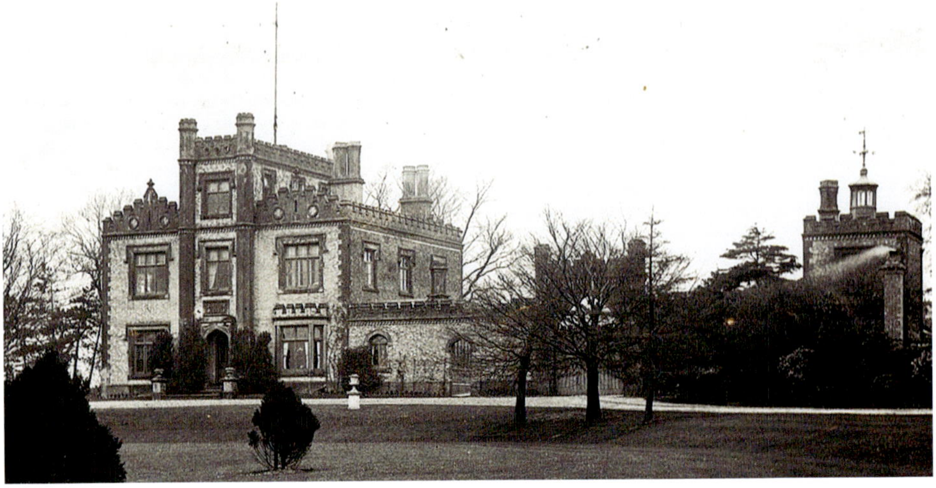

South-east view of Netherby Hall, from a postcard. (M. Craven)

was a low service wing and separate crenellated tower beyond all set in a neat small park. From its builder, William Haden, it passed to Maj. William Henry Haden VD (1860–1932), after whose death it became the home of Claude D. Dudley (1888–1943) and his wife Amy. After his death it failed to find a viable use and succumbed to the demand for housing *c.* 1959.

75. Penrhyn, Edgbaston, Warwickshire. *c.* 1960

A riot of Ruskinian Gothic, with bargeboarded gables, irregular façade, soaring brick chimneys and a richly elaborate interior, Penrhyn was built in Somerset Road, Edgbaston, in 1876 by (J. H.) Chamberlain & (W. H.) Martin for James Deykin. It was sold between 1908 and 1911 to a Mr Grey but by 1922 had

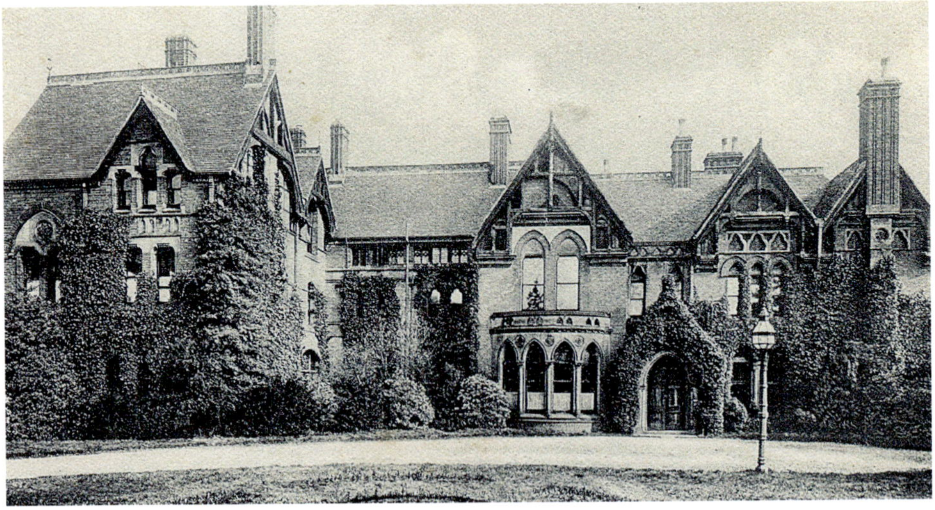

Penrhyn in 1907, from a postcard. (M. Craven)

become a Roman Catholic Retreat House. In 1926 it was adapted as a Catholic boys' school but, in 1941, was commandeered as a National Fire Service Auxiliary Fire Station C3 Y. After the war it became the property of the post office, surviving in use until the later 1950s, but was demolished in about 1960.

76. Highfield House, Halesowen, Worcestershire. 1961

Originally called Heckfield House, Highfield was a remarkable mid-eighteenth-century crenellated Gothic house, which until 1961 stood in Highfield Park. It was built of brick with stone dressings with some similarities to Speedwell Castle, Brewood, and much in the manner of Sanderson Miller. The four-bay façade, with three full-height canted bays, all with ogiform sashed fenestration, sitting on sill bands, topped with a modillion cornice supporting a crenellated parapet, appears like an applied façade, for behind there were bare brick elevations devoid of ornament. At the rear was a late eighteenth-century coach house capped by a bellcote containing a clock. The builder in 1757 was William Augustus Pitt (d. 1809), brother of the 1st Lord Rivers, on whose death it was let to Gen. Hon. Sir Lowry Cole. It was latterly the home of the Burr family, proprietors of the Hayseech Gun Barrel Works; tragically, two of the family's sons were killed in the First World War and the house was subsequently sold in 1920, after which it was the home of Revd Canon Colville, rector of Halesowen.

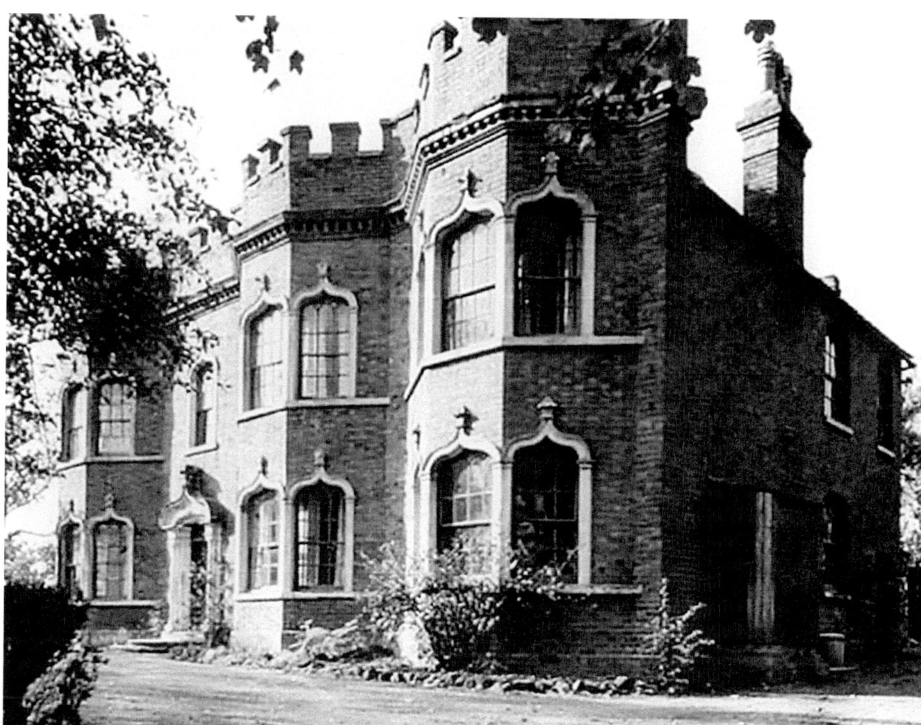

Highfield House photographed in 1960. (National Monuments Record)

77. Kingshurst Hall, Meriden, Warwickshire. 1962

Kingshurst Hall was a large, two-storey, red-brick building built on a medieval moated site in the very late seventeenth century, replacing a fortified house of fourteenth-century origin situated in the bailey of an earlier castle. By 1448 when it was the residence of Sir Edmund Montfort its surroundings had also been emparked. The Montforts sold in 1618 to Sir Richard Digby. The house was rebuilt for William Bull, whose family were tenants here for over 200 years. It probably had casement windows originally, those in the principal façade being replaced with sashes in the later eighteenth century; few other alterations to its fabric appear to have been made. To its rear was a group of early eighteenth-century subsidiary buildings, some of which were timber framed. The Bulls remained in residence until 1879 when they were succeeded by the Townsends. By this date the house's status had declined considerably, and in 1919 the freehold was sold but the Townsends remained as tenants. Two decades later, house and estate were purchased under a CPO by Birmingham Council and much of the estate developed for housing. The house fell into a state of disrepair in the 1950s when its then tenant, Walter Townshend, became unable to maintain it and moved out in 1960. By the time of its demolition in 1962 it was surrounded by tower blocks.

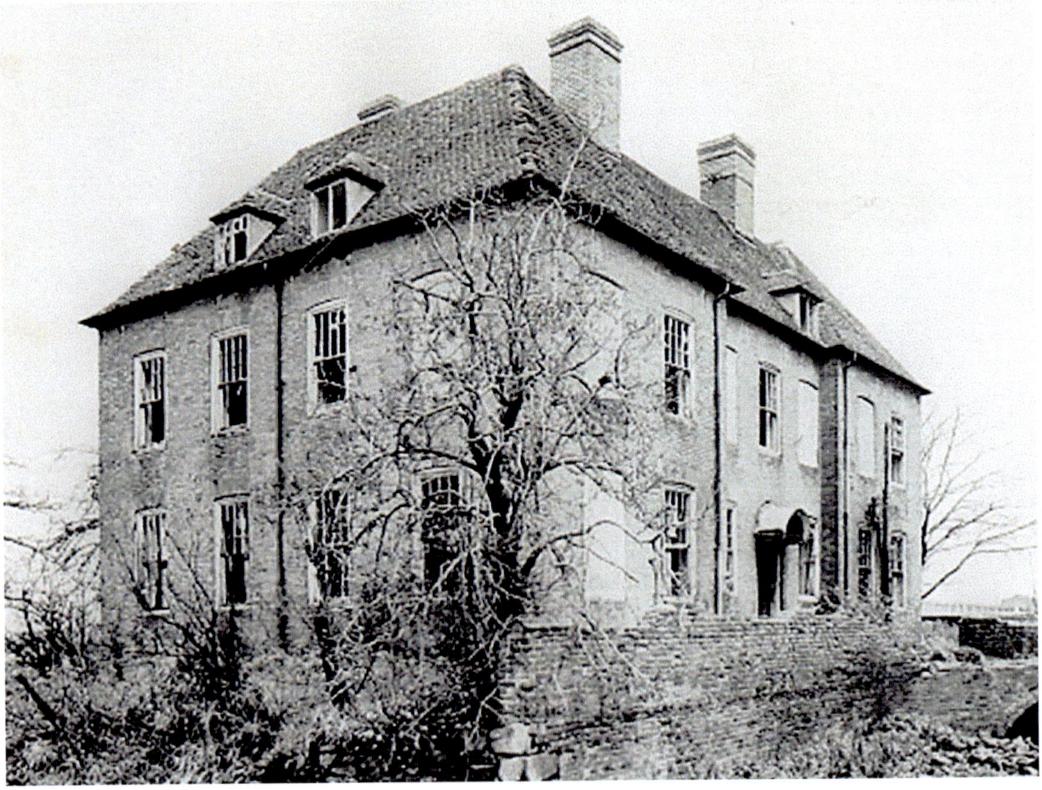

Kingshurst Hall shortly prior to demolition, 1961. (National Monuments Record)

78. Grove (The), Harborne, Warwickshire. 1963

The Grove was the home of social reformer and Birmingham's first Member of Parliament, Thomas Attwood. A painting in the collection of Birmingham Museums Trust shows a substantial pedimented Georgian stuccoed house on the site, but this was replaced for William Kenrick in 1877 by the architects Martin & Chamberlain. Its interiors, by J. H. Chamberlain, were richly Gothic, of which a superb Italianate Gothic antechamber originally located adjacent to the drawing room on the ground floor has been preserved in the Victoria & Albert Museum, London. The dining room, unlike the other interiors, was classical and top lit. The Kenricks presented both house and grounds to the city in the 1930s as Grove Park but continued to occupy the house until 1962. The house's contents were then sold, and it was demolished the following year. The lodge still stands at the park entrance, the park being open to the public.

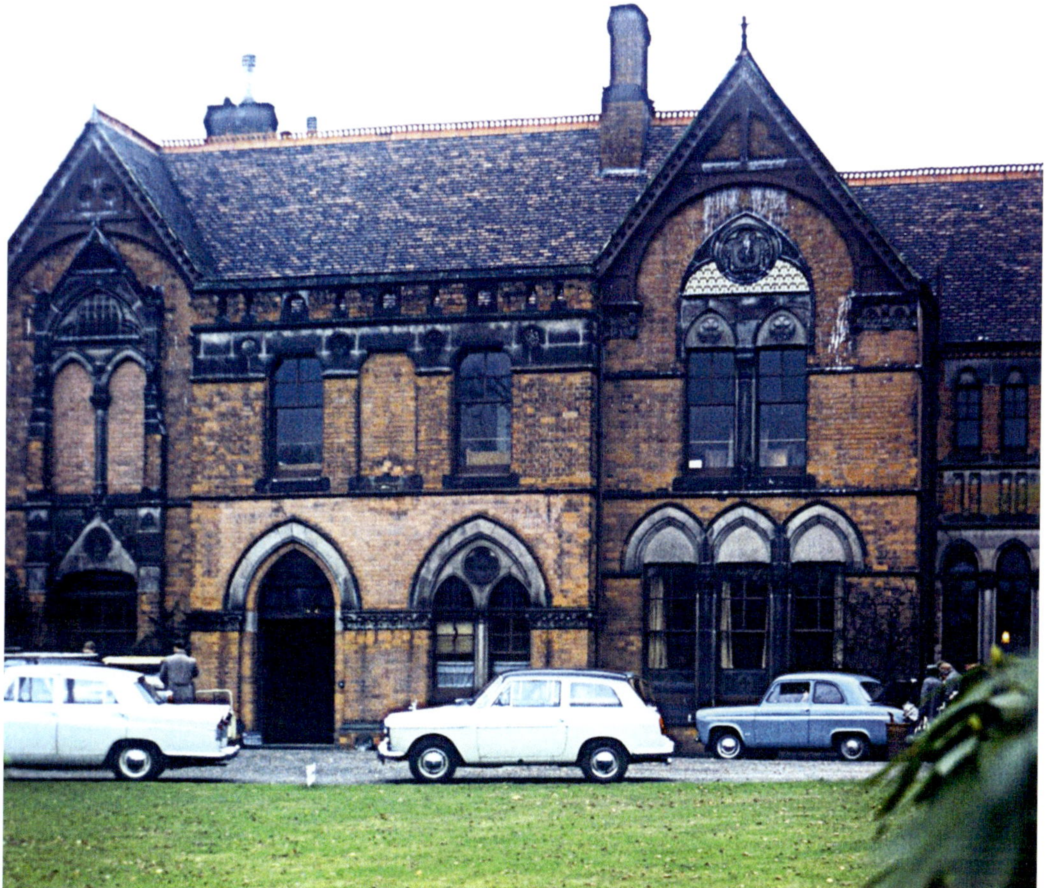

The Grove, Harborne, photographed by Phyllis Nicklin, 1961. (Creative Commons Lic Har0024)

79. Barnhurst Old Hall, Pendeford, Staffordshire. *c.* 1963

Barnhurst was held from the Levesons by the Cresswell family, Thomas Cresswell being recorded there in 1552. By the time Stebbing Shaw wrote in 1801, the old manor house was long gone, but he adds that 'amongst the remains of the old seat here is a square tower gateway with the date 1602 on it'. Towards the end of the same century Richard Cresswell replaced the old house with a well-proportioned six-bay, two-storey brick house with stone dressings under a hipped roof, although a low, double-pile range, part of its predecessor, was incorporated as a service wing. The original stone casement cross windows were later replaced with sashes. It was latterly known as Barnhurst Farm. Cresswell's posterity sold the estate to music collector and Handelian expert Sir Samuel Hellier (1737–84) of the Wodehouse, Wombourne, who allowed it to be tenanted as a farm. His heir was Revd Thomas Shaw, from 1786 Shaw-Hellier, whose widowed daughter-in-law Elizabeth died at the house in 1835, after which it reverted to being let as a farm. The estate was purchased by Wolverhampton Corporation in 1867, a sewage works being built in the house's grounds. After almost a century of desultory use, the gabled brick gatehouse was demolished in 1961, the house going two years later to make way for new houses. A fine octagonal dovecote which stood adjacent to the house survives.

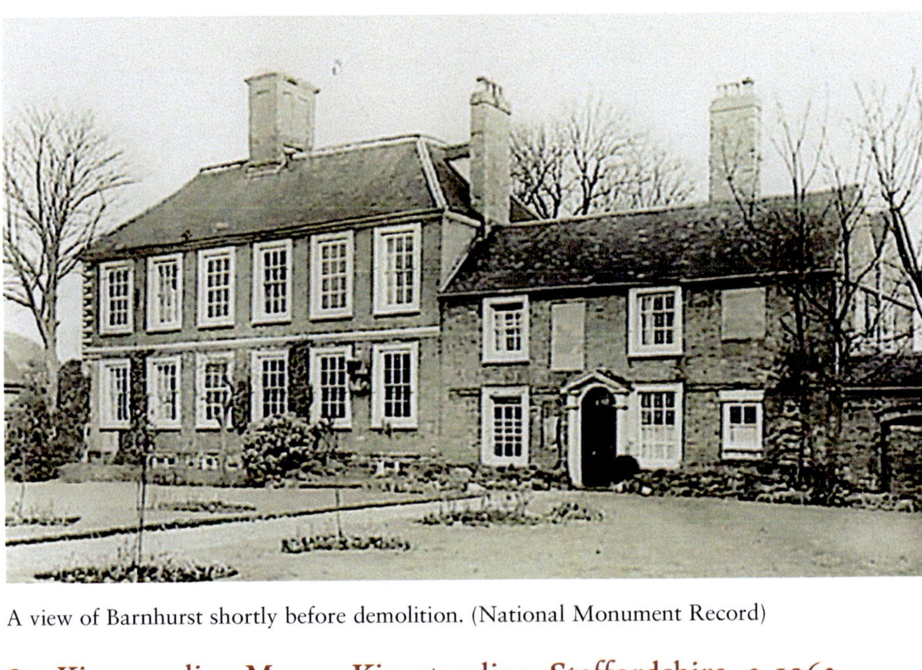

A view of Barnhurst shortly before demolition. (National Monument Record)

80. Kingstanding Manor, Kingstanding, Staffordshire. *c.* 1963

The manor house at Kingstanding in its later manifestations consisted of an eighteenth-century and older brick range, essentially a farmhouse, onto which was built, on land made available as a result of the 1824 enclosure award, a stuccoed two-storey Regency villa with a three-bay entrance front, first-floor sill band and a tetrastyle Doric portico. The two bay returns made an abrupt

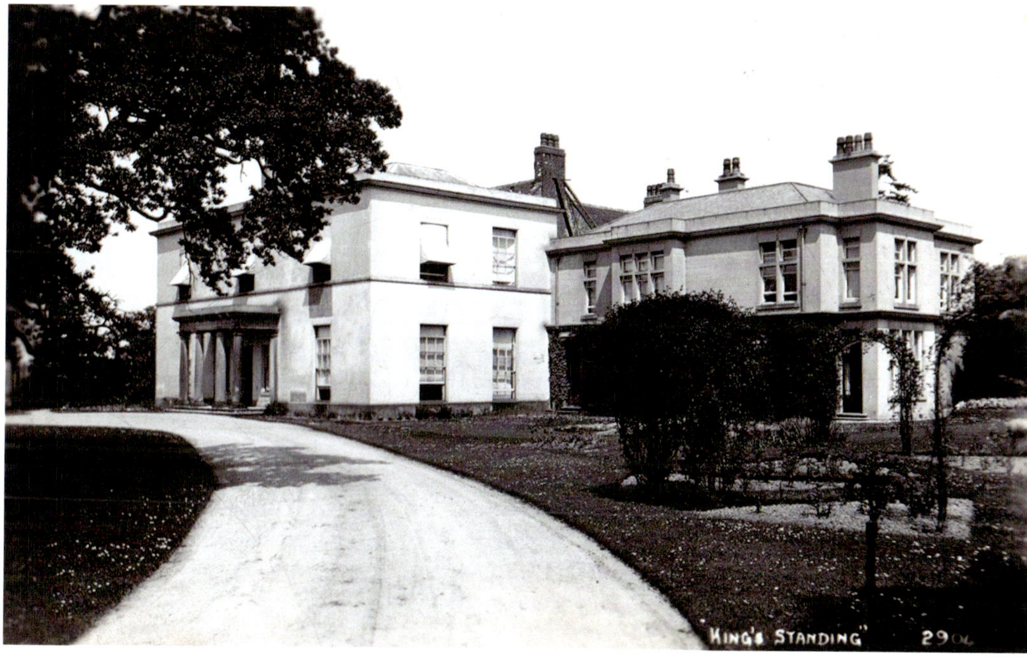

Kingstanding Manor, from a postcard, showing the later extension. (James Darwin)

join with the older portion. To this was added, in Victorian times, a lower two-storey wing with full-height canted bays to the south and east, mullioned windows with enhanced transoms, all under a low parapet and low hipped roof. Its demolition in *c*. 1963 was recorded by the Royal Commission on Historic Monuments.

81. Oakswell Hall, Wednesbury, Staffordshire. 1963

Oakswell was an engaging multi-period house with sixteenth-century origins, its predecessor in 1420 having been the seat of William Byng, whose family were followed by the Jennens. In its latter manifestation it had a lofty chamber storey, tallish brick diamond stacks, bunched in unlikely angles, a square tower with pyramidal roof and a later extension to the west. It appears to have been the creation of the Parkes family, who were there, according to the 1614 heralds' visitation, from the later sixteenth century, although one account would have Richard Parkes (d. 1729), by then a local coal owner, buying it in 1707. He left four daughters, dividing the patrimony, although the one who inherited the house married Sampson Lloyd, who made alterations (attic storey, re-fenestration) to enable it to be let it as a farm and exploited the minerals under the estate. The house was eventually sold by Parkes's posterity in 1874, when Joseph Smith, the first town clerk of Wednesbury, acquired and restored it, before selling to the town's chief medical officer, Walter Garman, in 1897. He sired a numerous and dysfunctional family and after his death in 1923, it was sold, passing through several hands prior to demolition during 1962–63.

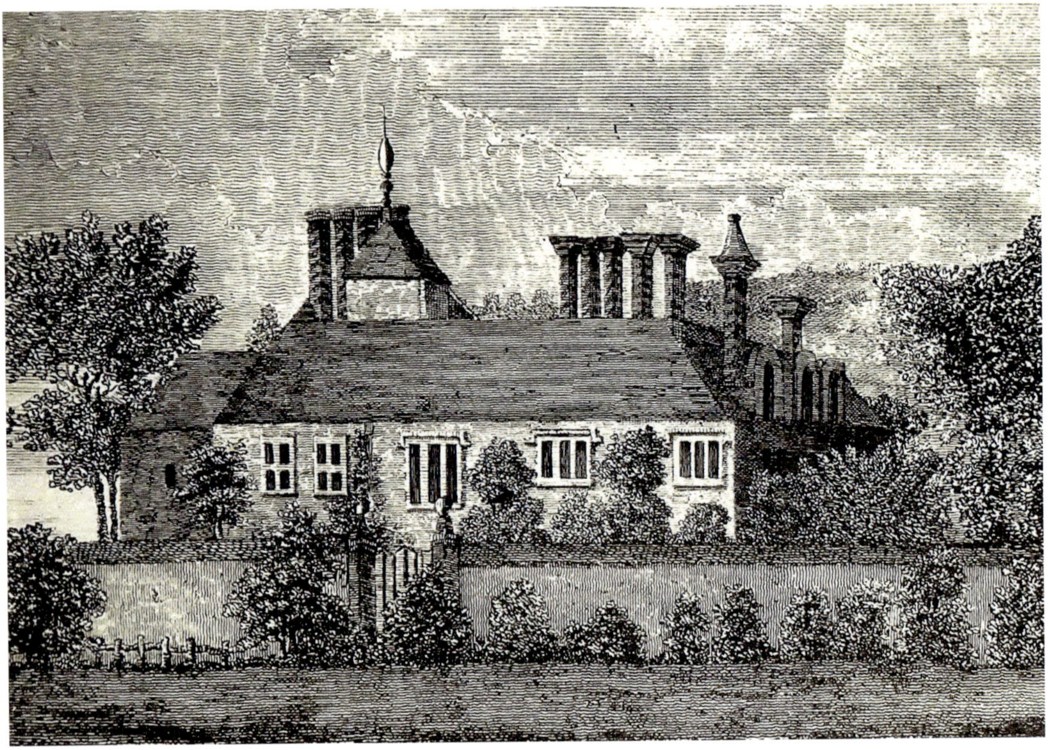

Oakswell Hall, from Stebbing Shaw, 1801. (M. Craven)

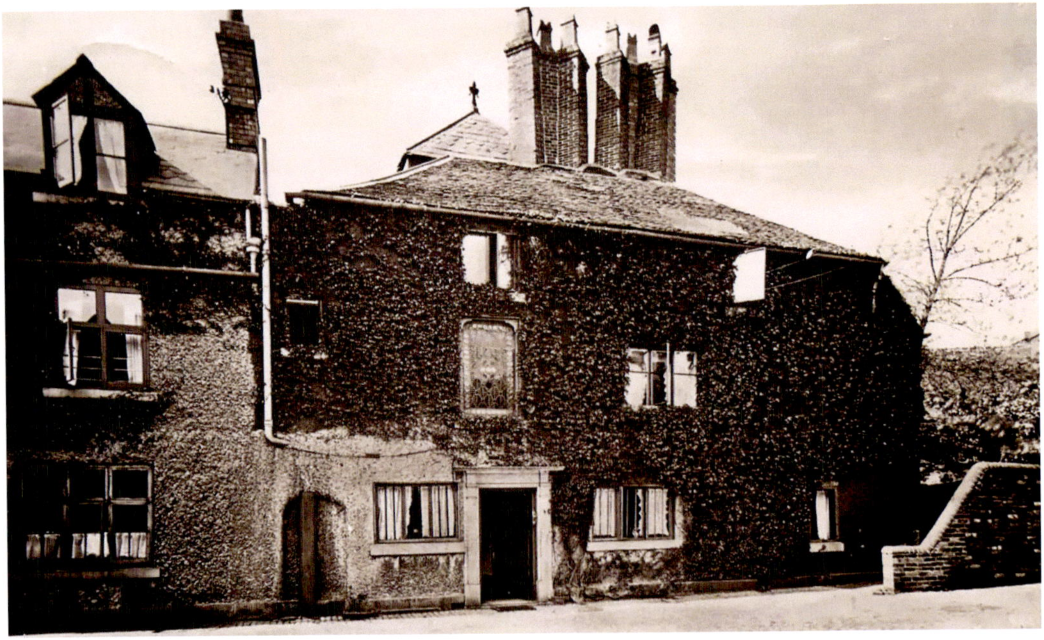

Oakswell Hall's entrance front, from a postcard, *c.* 1905. (James Darwin)

82. Ellowes Hall, Lower Gornal, Staffordshire. 1964

Ellowes was an exceptionally fine Regency villa built in a small park between 1821 and 1824 for opulent local ironmonger John Turton Fereday. It replaced (or was a rebuild of) an earlier house, which had been the home of the ironmaster Samuel Fereday. It was the only out-of-area house designed by the talented Barnstaple architect Thomas Lee and was a simplified version of Pyrland Hall, near Taunton (Somerset), of five by two bays, two and a half storeys, hipped roof behind a low parapet, with a rusticated ground floor, tetrastyle fluted Doric portico carrying an off first-floor loggia and recessed segmentally headed windows. The entrance hall had a screen of Ionic Scagliola columns and the drawing room ceiling was richly stuccoed. The relandscaping of the gardens was completed by 1826. The Feredays were there until 1851, by which time it had come to J. L. Bickley, who soon sold it

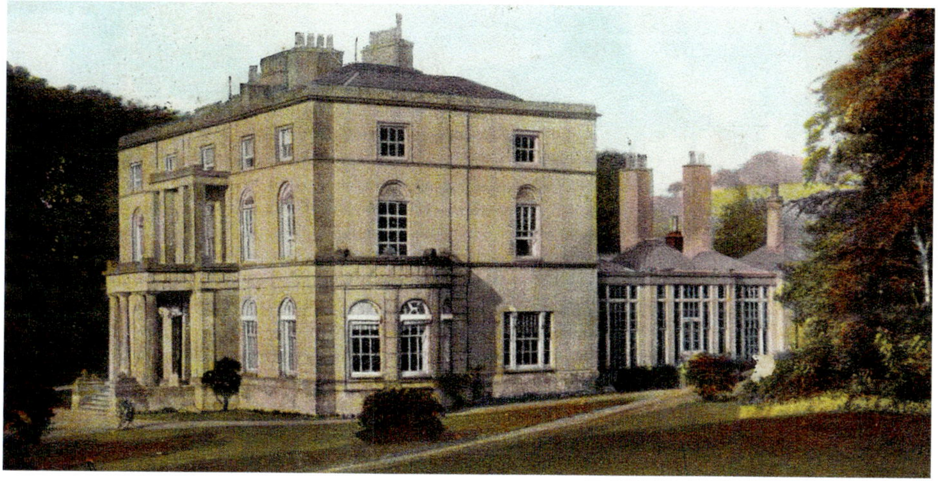

Ellowes from the south-east showing the conservatory, from a postcard of 1906. (M. Craven)

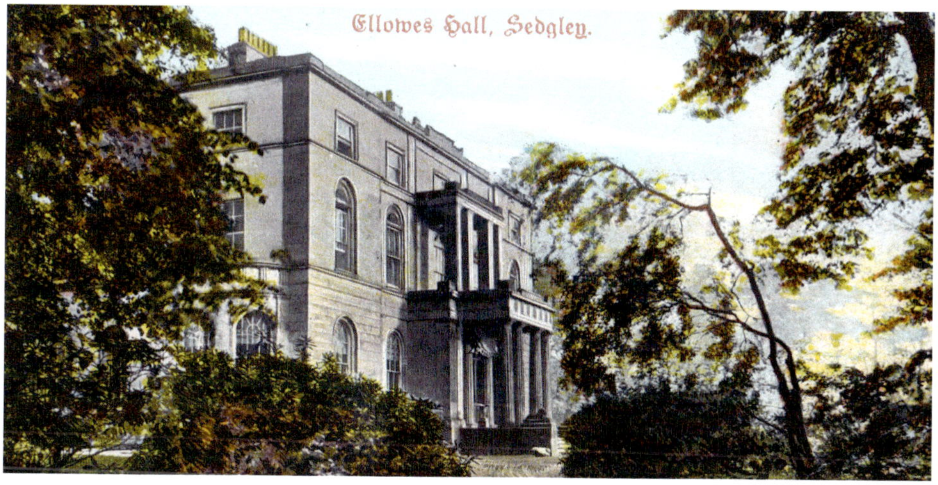

South-west view of Ellowes, from a postcard, *c.* 1907. (James Darwin)

on to William Baldwin. In 1865 it became the home of Charles Cochrane, mayor of Dudley, who was followed by Sir Horace St. Paul, 2nd Baronet, MP, who died there in 1891, aged seventy-nine. He was succeeded by Cllr. John Lloyd Gibbons, who died in 1919, when it was sold to the Mitchell family, but they were only there for four years before Henry Arthur Nock took up residence in 1923 and who also died there, in 1946, although during the war it had become a Home Guard HQ. The Nocks finally sold it in 1963 to the local education authority, who duly demolished it a year later.

83. Ashwood House, Kingswinford. Staffordshire. *c.* 1964

A large stuccoed classical mansion with stone dressings of probably late eighteenth-century origins, which belonged for most of its existence to the Himley Hall estate. It was the largest and one of the earliest of a group of impressive mansions constructed close to Summerhill, Kingswinford, most of which have since disappeared. In 1821 it was the home of Edward and Maria Dixon, for whom it appears to have been altered and extended. Edward Dixon was still in residence *c.* 1843. By 1845, however, it was occupied by the ironmaster John Joseph Bramah, who died here in 1848. From 1873 it was leased as a private asylum run by George Fowler Bodington and it remained an asylum until around the start of the Second World War. The house was one of the properties sold by the Earl of Dudley's Himley estate when it was broken up in 1947 and was empty at that time. According to the 1947 auction catalogue it had a fine staircase with mahogany balusters and an inlaid handrail.

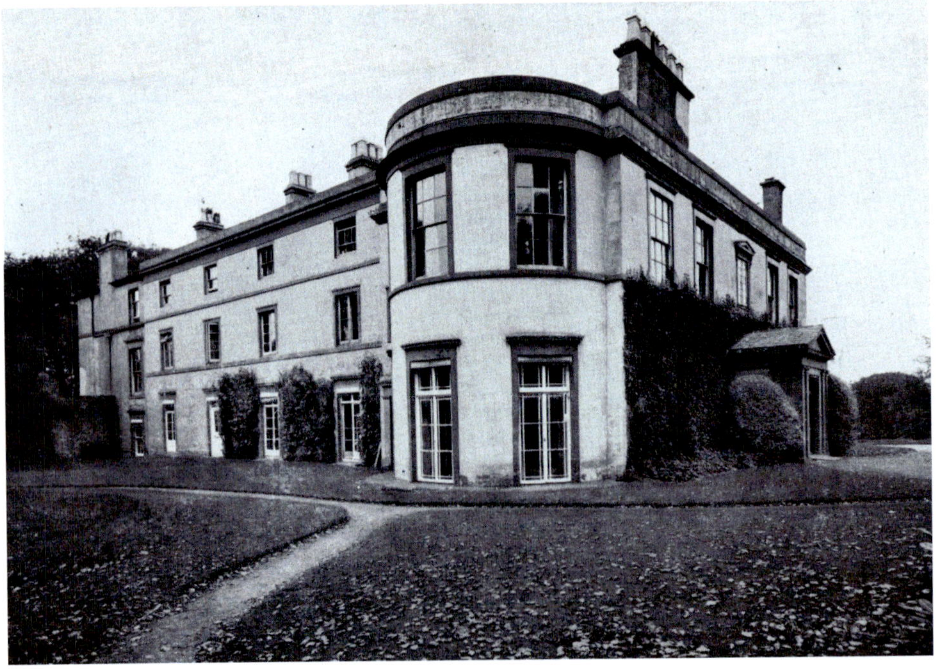

Ashwood House in 1947 from the estate auction catalogue. (James Darwin)

84. Endwood Court, Handsworth Wood, Staffordshire. 1965

Endwood Court was built for James Russell of the Crown Tube Works, Wednesbury, in 1838. It was reputedly designed by the talented Leamington Spa architect William Thomas and was built at a cost £7,000. Russell died at the house in 1849. Later nineteenth-century occupants included William Sharp JP, whose art collection there was auctioned after his death in 1881 by Christies, and later by Joseph Bennet Clarke. It was an elaborate, symmetrical, Gothic, stuccoed structure with a large Gothic conservatory. The house was much altered, shorn of much of its external decoration and considerably reduced in size by the Woodall family in the 1930s when it was converted into flats, but post-war the building became decrepit and the stucco was removed from the entrance front, which did not improve its resilience to the weather and, after a period lying empty from 1962 when Dares Estates Ltd bought it, the building was cleared three years later and the grounds redeveloped to be replaced by Endwood Court Road. Only the crenellated lodge remains.

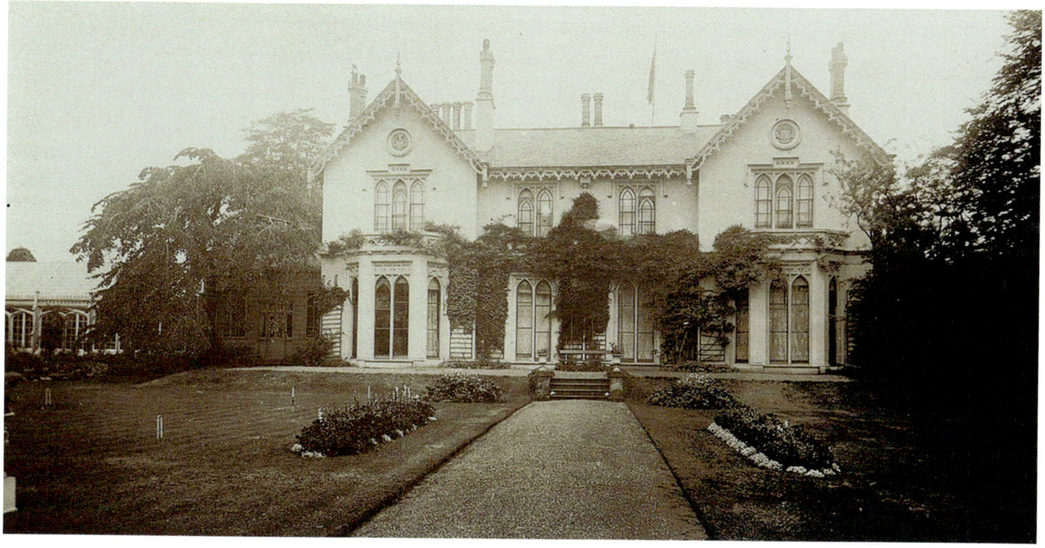

Endwood Court's garden front from a postcard of 1912. (M. Craven)

85. Henburys, Moseley, Worcestershire. 1965

There was a house on the site from the seventeenth century and by the early nineteenth century, it stood within 45 acres of park and farmland with an obelisk forming an eye-catcher. When sold in 1826, the estate included a new built stable block and coach house, hot houses, farm buildings and a separate farmhouse. The classical house must have primarily dated from after that date and was designed to exploit views over the Lickey Hills. It was occupied by the silver plater Charles Rotheram *c.* 1837 through the 1840s. From 1840, its estate was bisected by the Birmingham & Gloucester Railway (Midland Railway from 1848), resulting in the home farm being rebuilt to the north of the track after that date. To compensate for the loss of land the estate was expanded westwards

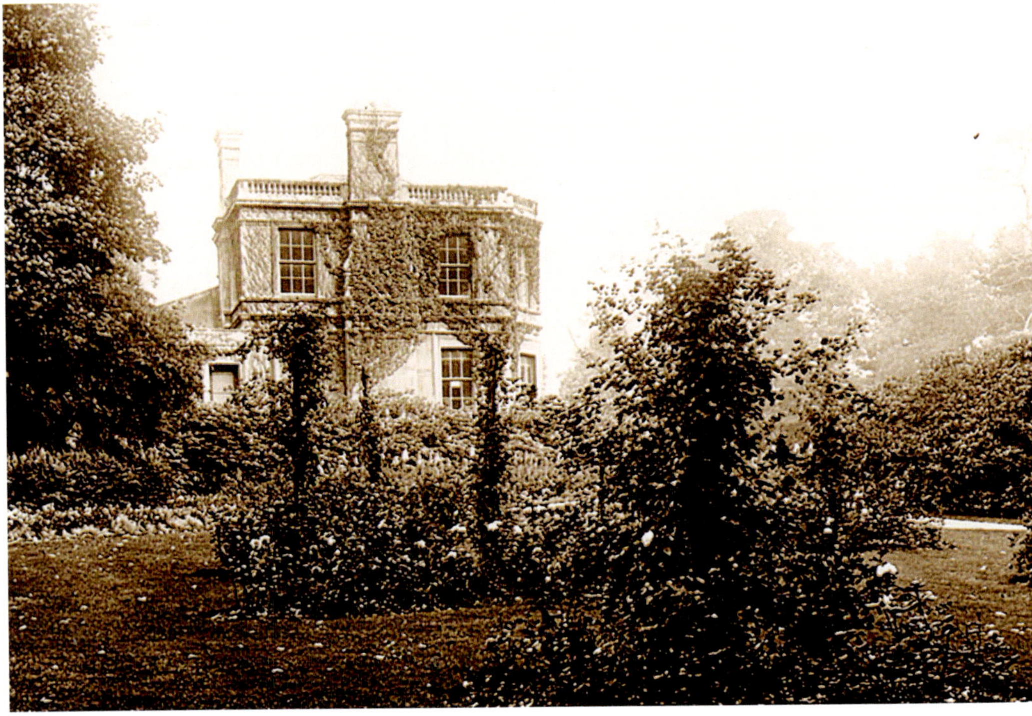

The remaining portion of Henburys standing in Uffculme Park, *c.* 1931, from a postcard. (M. Craven)

to form a park of over 60 acres. The house was occupied by the Lyndons, edge tool manufacturers, from the 1850s until the time of its demolition. G. F. Lyndon extended the house to the designs of Thomas Plevins in 1876. The family, however, became increasingly concerned about suburban encroachment and sold the estate in 1895. Most of the house was demolished that year, along with many of its garden structures when the estate was absorbed into the grounds of Richard Cadbury's Uffculme. 42 acres of the Henbury estate were then let to the Chamberlains of Highbury. The remaining two-storey section of the house was later used as refreshment rooms for what became Uffcombe Park. This sad remainder of the building disappeared *c.* 1965.

86. Wollescote House, Stourbridge, Worcestershire. 1965

This was originally a timber-framed house adjoining the Millward estate at Wollescote Hall. It was purchased by the Millward family in 1750 to extend their estate. The date of building is unclear, but it was clearly a substantial and distinguished stuccoed Regency neoclassical house of two storeys and nine bays, with a Doric porch flanked by tripartite windows, beyond which, either side, three bays broke forward under a pediment. Thomas Badger acquired the house in 1851, which passed to his son-in-law T. H. Pargeter, who died in 1880. It was then sold or let to George Taylor, who was followed by Frederick James in 1901, before it was bought in 1912 by Charles Howell, a director of the Hartshill Iron

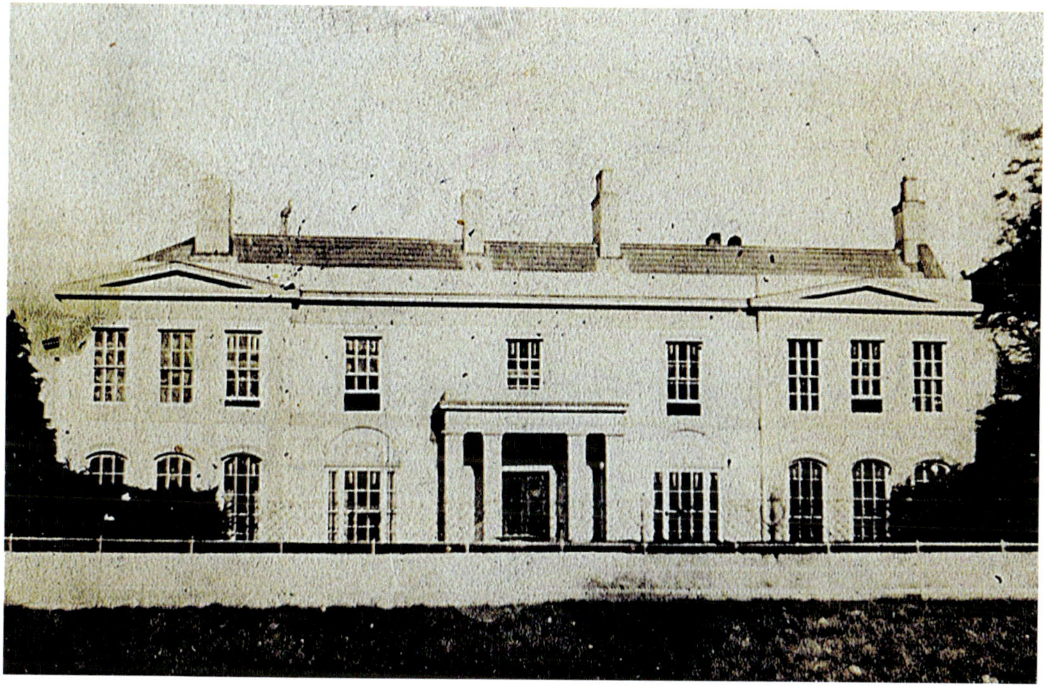

Wollescote House's entrance front in 1886. (James Darwin)

Company; his daughter, the celebrated pianist Dorothy Howell, grew up here. The house and grounds, along with Wollescote Hall, were purchased in 1930 by Ernest Stevens (1867–1957) as part of his subsequent gift of a park to the people of Lye and Wollescote. Unfortunately, Wollescote House failed to find a viable role, and was demolished in 1965, although the earlier hall survived.

87. Prescot House, Lye, Worcestershire. 1968

A late eighteenth-century red-brick villa which is shown as a two-storey, five-bay, pedimented structure on a drawing of 1828. It was possibly built for Aaron Attwood in the 1790s and replaced an earlier house, but by 1828 it was the home of the banker and manufacturer Francis Rufford, who died there in 1831. He was followed by his son, also Francis and an MP, who greatly altered and extended the house before being declared bankrupt in 1851. It later passed to the Holcrofts, fire brick manufacturers. Prescot House was again altered and extended after 1912 for the manufacturer Ernest Stevens. The house's most impressive internal feature was a top-lit staircase hall with Ionic marble columns and an elaborate wrought-iron balustrade. Other rooms contained Edwardian panelling and chimneypieces. Its gardens were extensive and included a fernery, palm house, walled garden and a Doric garden temple. Stevens died in 1957, and the house's contents were then sold. From 1958 to 1965 it became the home of Queen's College but in was cleared in 1968 to be replaced by housing.

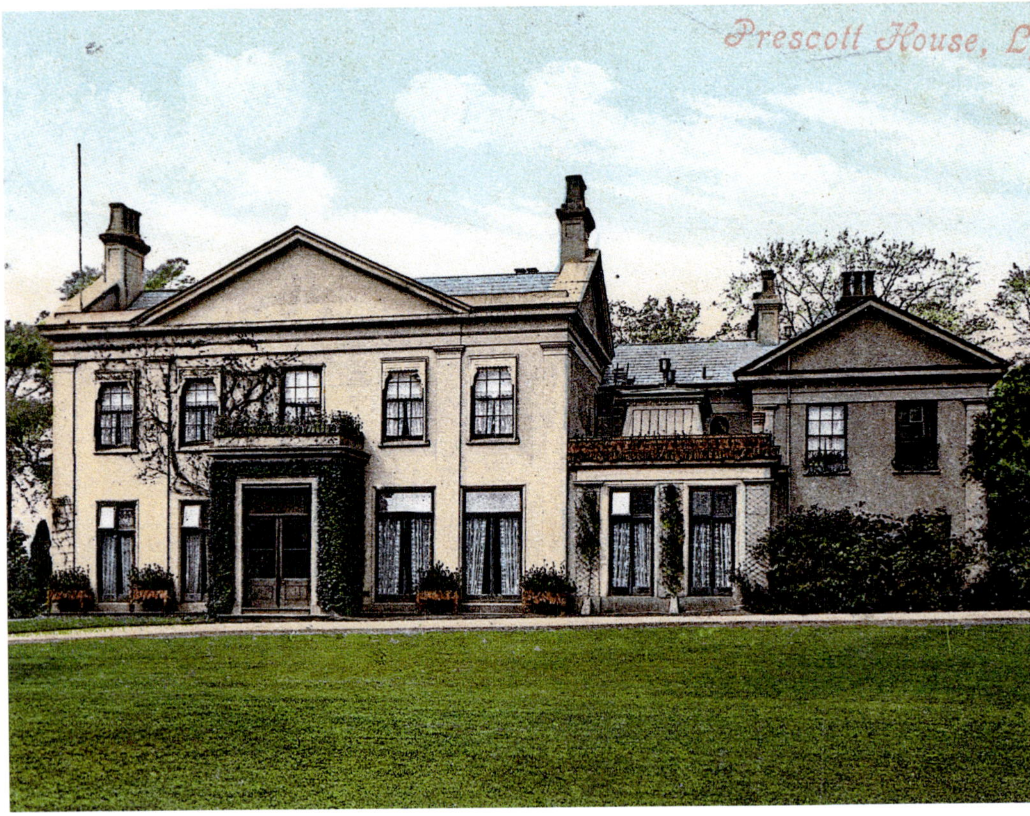

Prescot House depicted on a postcard of 1908. (James Darwin)

88. Townsend House, Sedgley, Staffordshire. *c.* 1968

Whilst the origin of its name would appear somewhat opaque, the house itself was built shortly after the Restoration by Richard Wilkes, third in descent from William Wilkes who was of Willenhall in the sixteenth century. It had a triple-gabled, two-storey garden façade, which was in the Victorian era extended by one bay at each end, whilst there were considerable extensions at the rear, latterly all stuccoed and the entrance front given a gabled façade to reflect the garden façade. Wilkes' heir was his nephew Richard Wilkes, his cousin once removed, but he sold to John Badley (1678–1762). It later came back into the hands of the Wilkes family, until farmer and bedstead manufacturer George Frederick Wilkes (1866–1942) sold Townsend House to Roger Shawe Maley TD between 1911 and 1936, who let it as a prep school. When this failed about 1960, the house was unoccupied for a time before being demolished for house building in 1968, a stretch of the stone perimeter wall surviving between Townsend Avenue and High Park Crescent, Sedgley, defining part of the grounds.

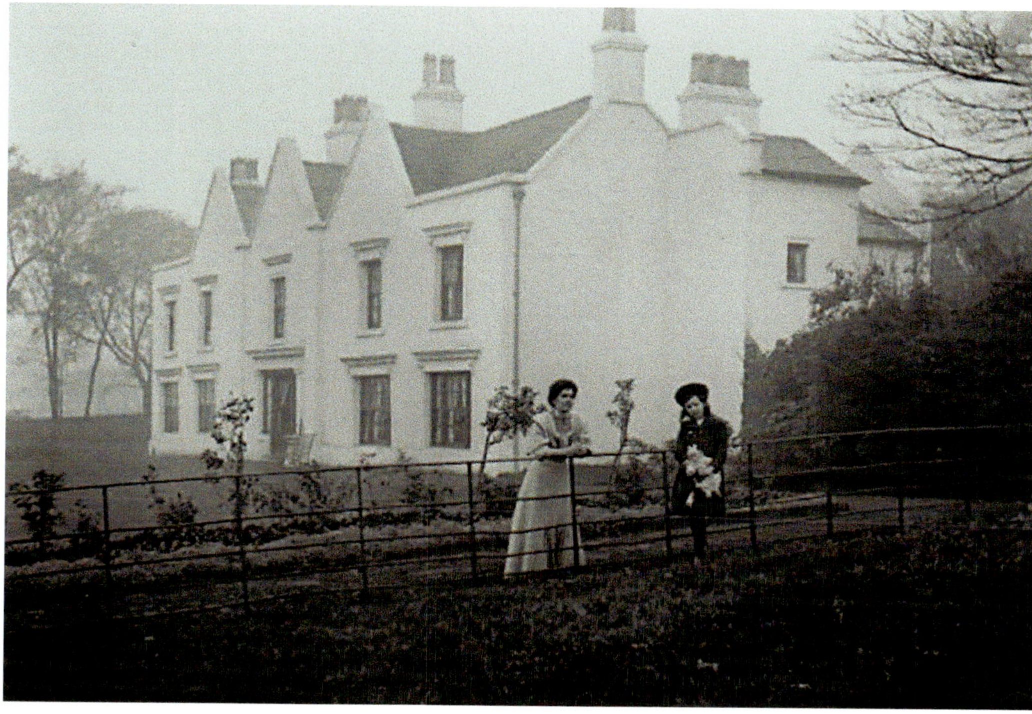

Townsend House, a family album view of 1908. (Private collection)

89. Tettenhall Wood House, Wolverhampton, Staffordshire. 1969

Tettenhall Wood was a Regency Gothic villa of two storeys and a slightly asymmetrical six bays with a central octagonal entrance tower of three storeys and a stair turret, all with sill bands, Gothic tracery and a crenellated parapet, built between 1831 and 1833 by Thomas Rickman for Theodosia Hinckes to replace an earlier house which had been purchased by the family in the 1770s. It stood within 91 acres of parkland, which formed part of a larger 390-acre estate. The staircase hall contained a fine stair with crenellated newels and a window containing late medieval Flemish stained glass related to the de Croÿ family, from the Church of Our Lady, Aarschot. Miss Hinkes died in 1874, bequeathing the house to the Archdeacon of Stafford for life, but by the late 1890s it had been sold to the Bayliss family, iron founders, and then in 1912 to the Hickmans, the parkland largely being sold for development in the mid-1950s, leaving only 17 acres. The house and remaining land were sold to Tarmac Ltd in 1964 for £85,000 with the provision that Ethel Hickman could continue living there until her death. Much to the Tarmac directors' consternation, she lived to 103, dying in 1969. The house was then quickly demolished, although the architect Keith Cattell saved the dining room window, now a folly in his garden. A *cottage ornée* lodge survives, whilst other decorative work went to Australia. The remaining parkland was immediately developed for housing.

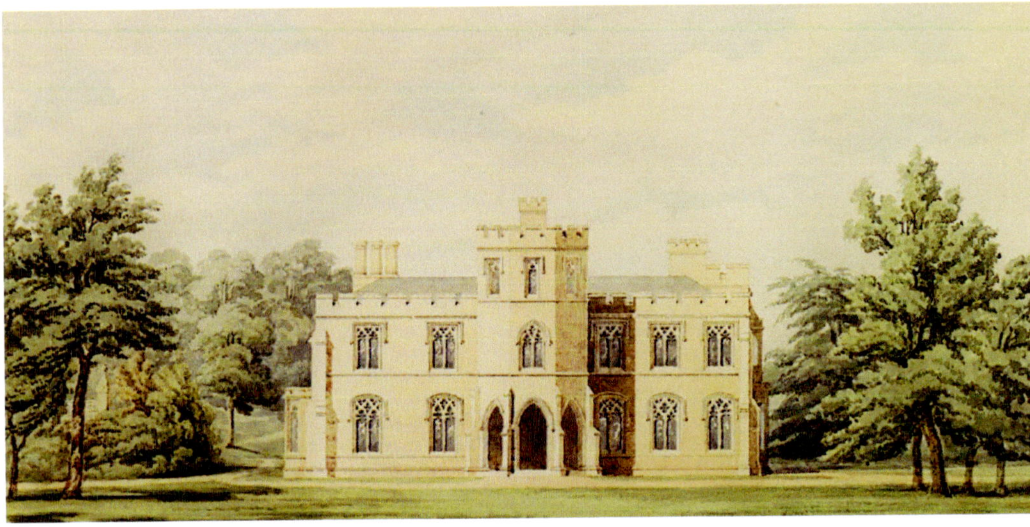

Tettenhall Wood – Thomas Rickman's 1831 elevation. (RIBA)

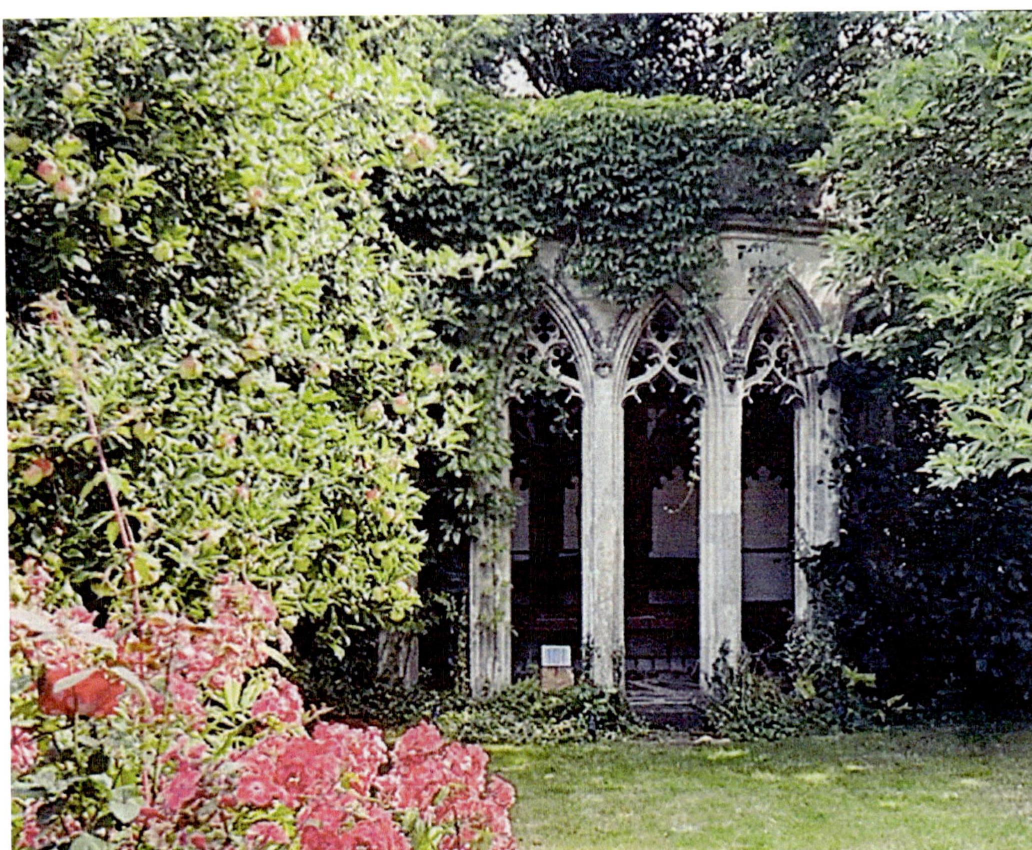

Tettenhall Wood, dining room window in Mr Cattell's garden. (Private collection)

90. Park Hall, Castle Bromwich, Warwickshire. *c.* 1970

The medieval moated seat of the Arden family, relatives of Mary Arden, Shakespeare's mother, was replaced by a new house after the Restoration, of brick with a tall three-bay centre flanked by two-bay, slightly projecting cross wings embellished with shaped gables. Part of the earlier house was retained, attached to the south-east angle and suitably refreshed. The estate passed out of the Arden family in 1643 after the death of Robert Arden from smallpox. Thus it seems likely that this new house was built for his brother-in-law Sir Herbert Price, 1st Baronet (1605–78), or his son, Sir Thomas Arden Price, 2nd Baronet. After 1704 it became part of the Castle Bromwich Hall estate and became a farmhouse, being eventually demolished around the time of the construction of the M6 motorway (1970), when the area was developed for housing, by which time it had become derelict. Part of its estate is now a nature reserve.

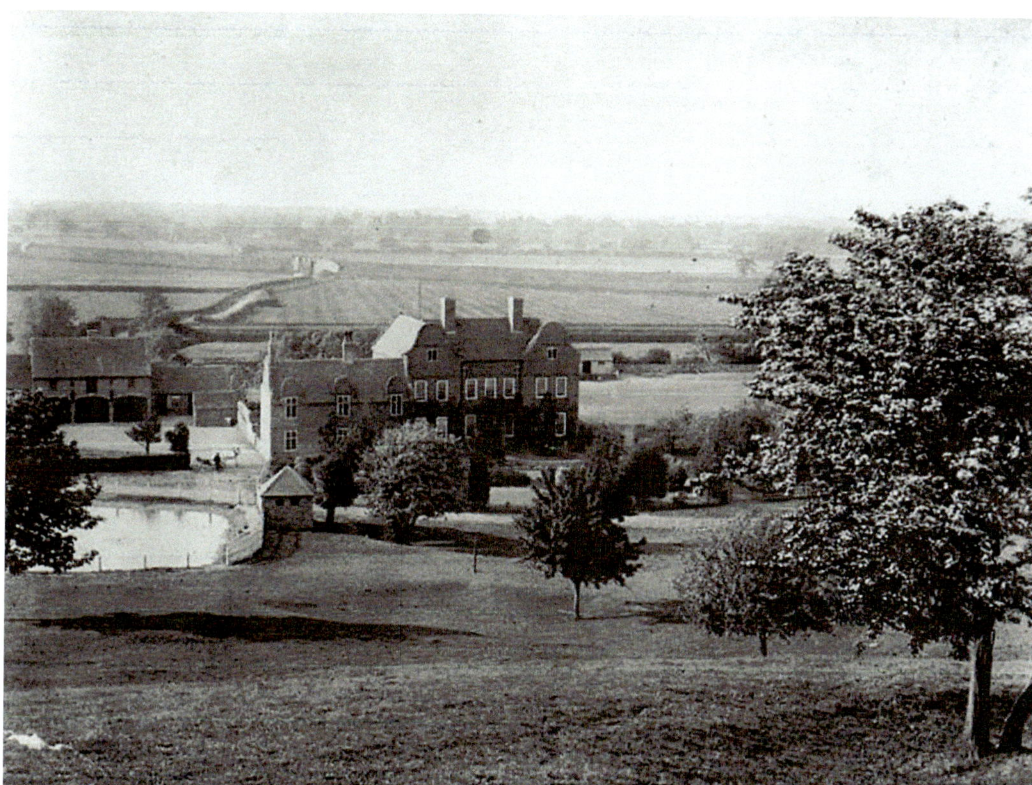

Park Hall seen from the east in the 1930s – a rural idyll. (Private collection)

91. Moor Green House, Moseley, Worcestershire. 1970

Moor Green was built for Henry Charles Holder and his new wife Evelyn to replace a smaller but still substantial house given to him with 13 acres of land by his father, the brewer Sir John Holder, in 1899. Both the house and land had formerly been part of his father's adjoining Pitmaston House estate. The new

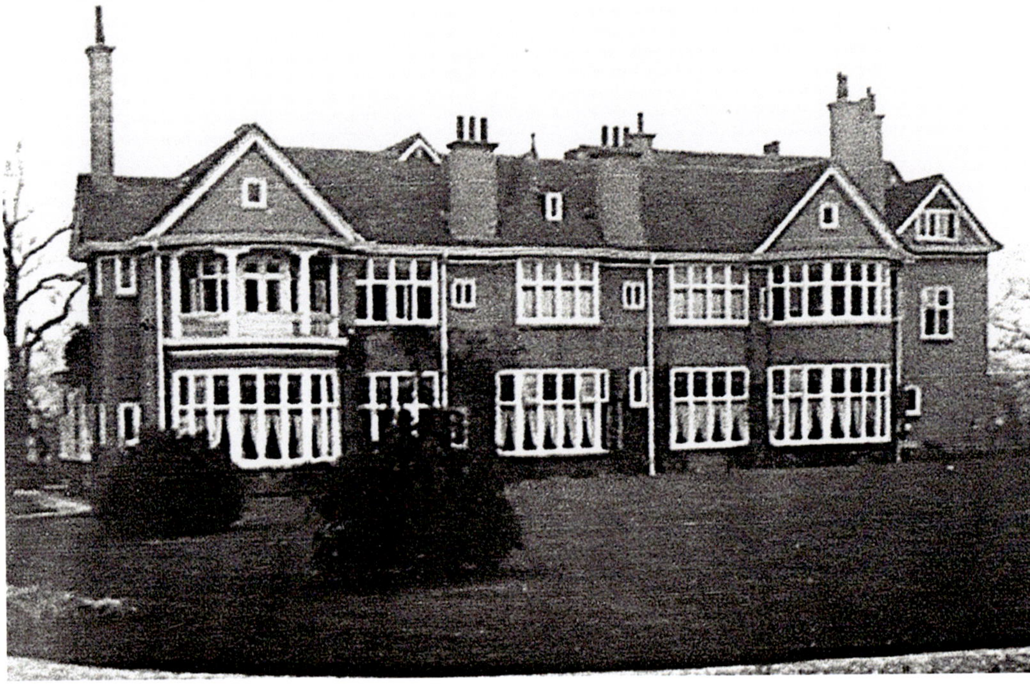

Moor Green House, Moseley, in 1912. (Private collection)

house was designed by the Birmingham architect William Henman FRIBA, a pioneer in the early use of concrete and in the ventilation of buildings. It was a sprawling building constructed at a cost £8,000 and was built with such modern luxuries as a lift, a photographic dark room, its own generator and motor garages. There was also stabling, farm buildings, a peach house, conservatories, a walled garden and a full-sized tennis court, some possibly surviving from the earlier house. The entrance front was in an eclectic, if subdued, Tudor vernacular style, whilst its garden façade incorporated Queen Anne Revival detailing. By the time of its completion it was already something of an anachronism as the neighbouring estate was already beginning to sell land for building. It was seldom occupied and by 1912 the house and its park were for sale, with half of the parkland being advertised seperately as building plots. By 1918 it had become an auxilliary hospital but in 1920 it was purchased for use as a works social club for Britannic Assurance, offices being built in the park. The firm demolished the old house in 1970 to extend its offices.

92. Duddeston House, Aston, Warwickshire. 1971

The Holte family held Duddeston with Nechells and Aston from the fourteenth century and had a seat at Duddeston within a moat. However, once Aston Hall

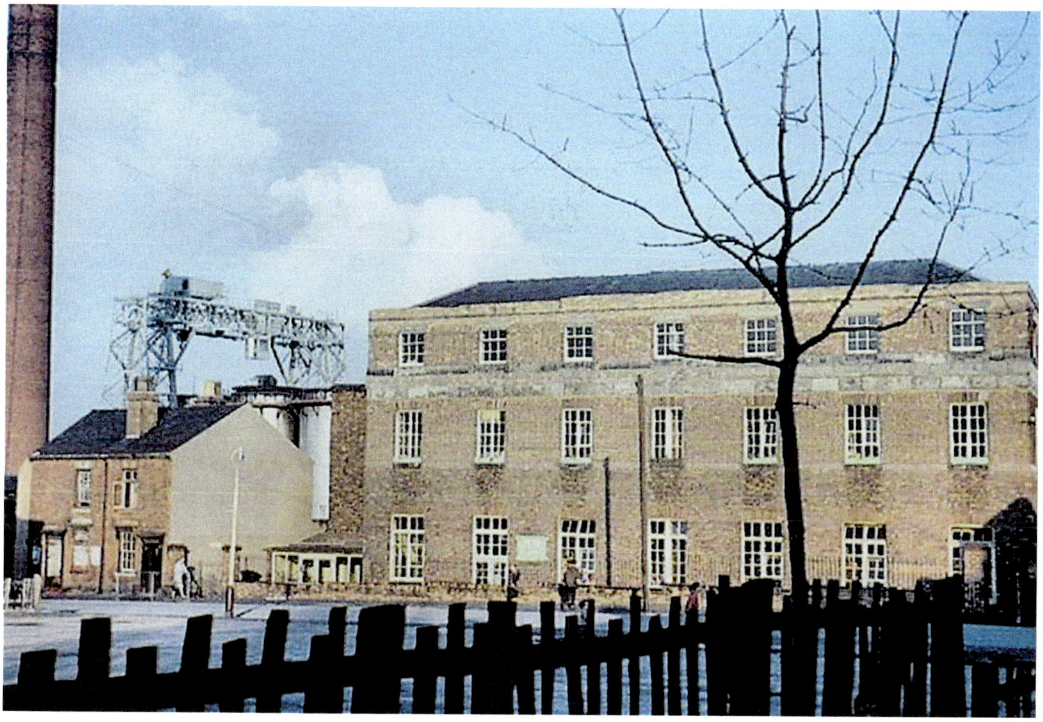

Duddeston House's garden front, in 1954, with the Saltley gasworks blighting the scene. (Phyllis Nicklin via Keith Berry)

was complete, the Holtes left Duddeston in 1631 and let it. In the early eighteenth century Andrew Butler refronted or refaced the house in brick with two storeys, attic above the cornice, and a double-pile range attached to the garden front. In 1750 the former pleasure grounds were relandscaped and opened to the public as a place of resort in imitation of and named after London's Vauxhall Gardens. And whilst the house was ultimately demolished in 1781, the gardens survived into the early twentieth century before being closed and sold for housing development. Samuel Galton Sr, availing himself of 12 acres of the grounds by the river in 1758, built a new house of brick, very plain, of seven bays and two storeys, with attics above the cornice and a hipped roof. For the son, Samuel Galton FRS (1753–1832), Robert Lugar designed a fishing temple and probably added the portico. Behind the principal range early engravings show a substantial projecting lower wing. Subsequent Galtons preferred to live at The Larches, Sparkbrook (q.v.). In 1838 it was let as a lunatic asylum 'of high respectability', on the grounds that 'no one in his senses would live in it'. This closed in 1868, whereupon it became St Anne's National School, heavily altered and stripped of its external ornament, whilst its parkland became the site of a railway sidings and Saltley gasworks. In its final days it was hemmed in by buildings on Devon Street and the school closed and the house finally demolished as part of an urban clearance scheme in 1971.

93. Portway House, Rowley Regis, Staffordshire. 1977

Portway House, or (Old) Hall, was dated 1672 on a panel over the entrance, accompanied by what appeared to be the head and shoulders of a judge. It was of a type of lodge common in the mid-seventeenth century and closely resembled the hall at Butterton (qv *Lost Houses of Staffordshire*) and Stydd Hall at Yeaveley (Derbyshire). That said, what sources there are suggest it was originally timber framed and was stuccoed in the early nineteenth century, which seems less convincing when one looks at the surviving photographs, and an early nineteenth-century view in the Pardoe Collection of the Georgian Group shows it as in the postcard view of 1905 here, and it clearly had received a mildly Gothic makeover to its entrance and the ramped wing to the left. The upper-floor windows, five light mullioned windows, the projecting full-height porch, parapet and crenellations all seem convincing for the date. Inside were a 'wide oak staircase' and decoratively plastered ceilings. In the nineteenth century, ironmasters James and Thomas Williams were there and doubtless provided the makeover; by the early twentieth century it was farmed by Enoch Richards, followed by Samuel Chapman and in the 1930s by David Pardoe. It was – astoundingly – never listed and was demolished in 1977 due to mining subsidence, but was recorded by Dan Cruikshank that year.

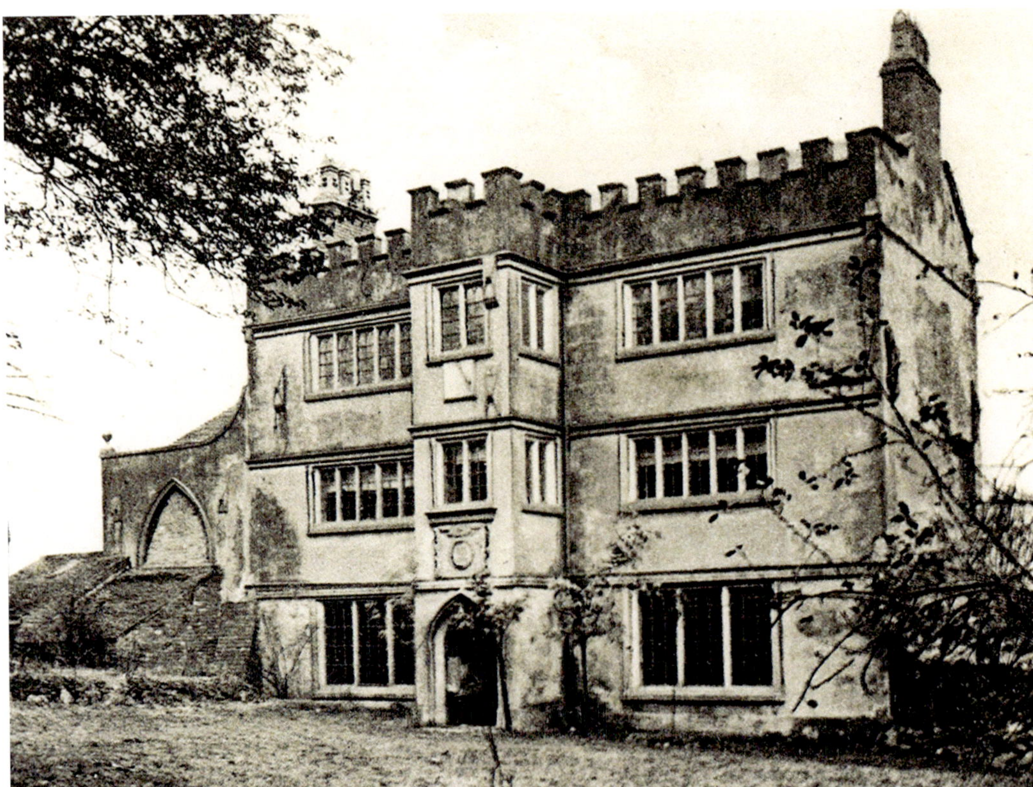

Portway Old Hall, 1903, from a postcard. (M. Craven)

94. Monkspath Hall, Shirley, Warwickshire. 1980

Built *c.* 1775, this brick, five-bay, two-storey villa with a high hipped roof with attic dormers and central entrance was altered in the mid-nineteenth century when canted ground-floor bays and a heavy Italianate porch were added and the sash windows replaced with plate glass. In 1799 it was the seat of Richard Burman, but by the 1830s it was the home of Mary Ann Cary, who was succeeded by W. S. Colemore. Latterly it became a farmhouse, tenanted by the Bickford family. Despite being Grade II listed, it was demolished without consent by the driver of a contractor's bulldozer on a bank holiday, who claimed that he had made a mistake over which building he was supposed to be bulldozing (and was duly fined heavily). It was then ordered to be rebuilt but the unconvincing replica was delisted in 1990 and is now divided as flats.

95. Berry Hall (New Berry Hall) Solihull, Warwickshire. 1990

Berry Hall was gabled neo-Tudor brick mansion designed by J. A. Chatwin in 1875 for Joseph Gillott (1826–1903), a pen manufacturer who had purchased the estate, along with the previous timber-framed house (which was kept, and survives as Old Berry Farm) in 1867. It had a tower, the design of which was based on that of the Tom Tower at Christ Church, Oxford. The internal decoration was by Lamb & Co. and there was stained glass supplied by Hardman. The estate was sold in 1904 to William Upton, who shot himself in the porch in 1908, but his widow lived on at the house until 1938. The house was then sold to Harold Tippetts, who refurbished it, but it became derelict after 1957 when it was sold to developers and gradually fell into ruin, being demolished in spring 1990. Two Grade II lodge houses and gates survive.

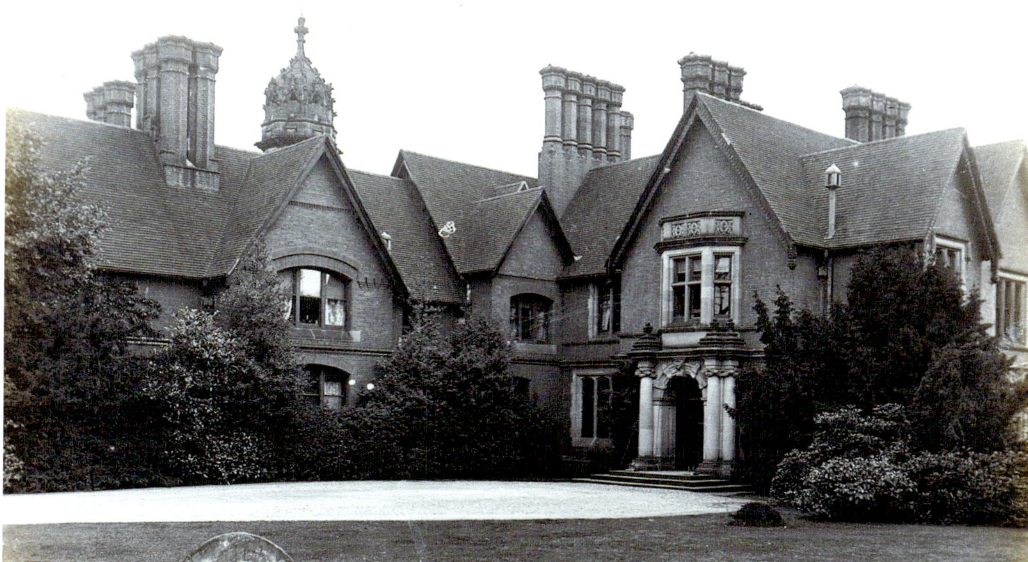

Berry Hall, 1930s. (James Darwin)

96. Summerhill Court, Kingswinford, Staffordshire. 1992

Summerhill Court was a mid-Victorian irregular gabled, red-brick, neo-Tudor mansion with stone dressings, which was built in about 1860, the last of the group of distinguished mansions to be built in this area of Kingswinford. It was the seat of Herman Smith, an iron founder. The estate passed by marriage to Colonel David Lewis but was sold in 1911 to the colliery owner Harry Sidney Pitt and his wife Martha. The widowed Martha Pitt died at the house in 1948. Its grounds were then gradually developed for housing, and the empty house slowly became derelict, finally being demolished in 1992.

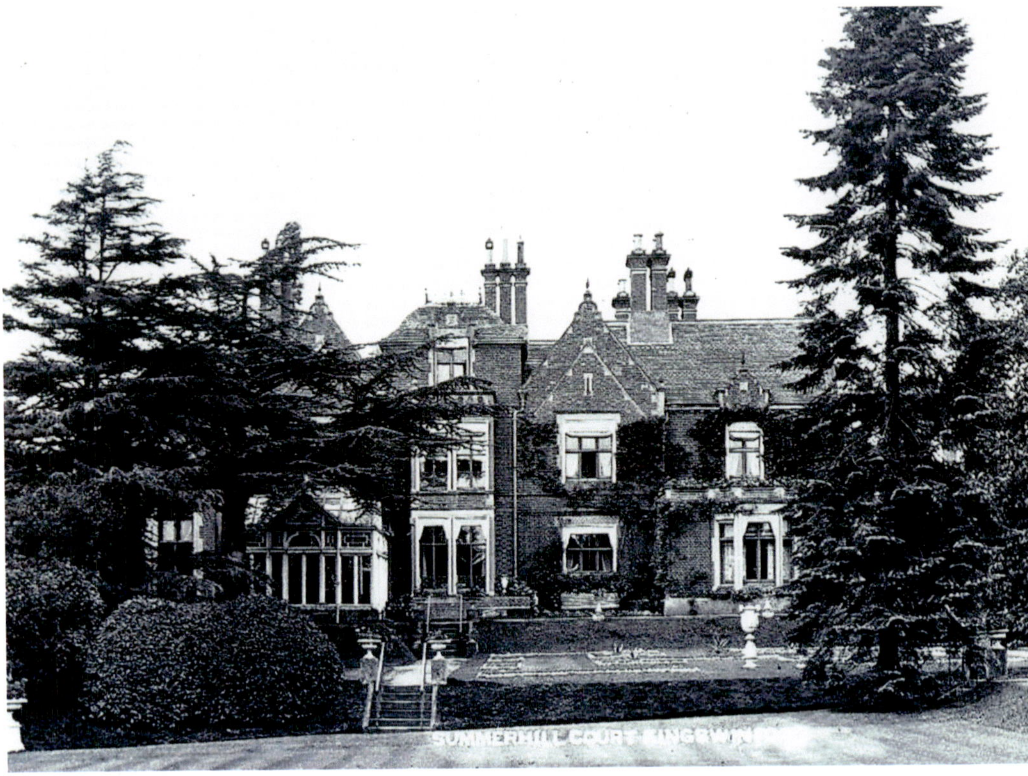

Summerhill Court, from a postcard. (James Darwin)

97. Fowgay Hall, Solihull, Warwickshire. 2007

Fowgay Hall or Bo(w)gay Hall stood at the corner of what is now Whitfields Road and Dingle Lane and reputedly dated from 1699, although the VCH suggests its origins went back to the early Tudor period. What survived at the time of demolition was possibly the wing of a much larger house which had been converted as a farm. It had been greatly altered and extended in 1883 (dated on chimney breast) when canted bay windows were also added to its garden façade and the chimneys rebuilt. Henry White was in residence from the end of the nineteenth century until the First World War. In the 1930s it was a school run by Mr and Mrs Callaghan, but this moved premises in 1940 and Fowgay once again became a

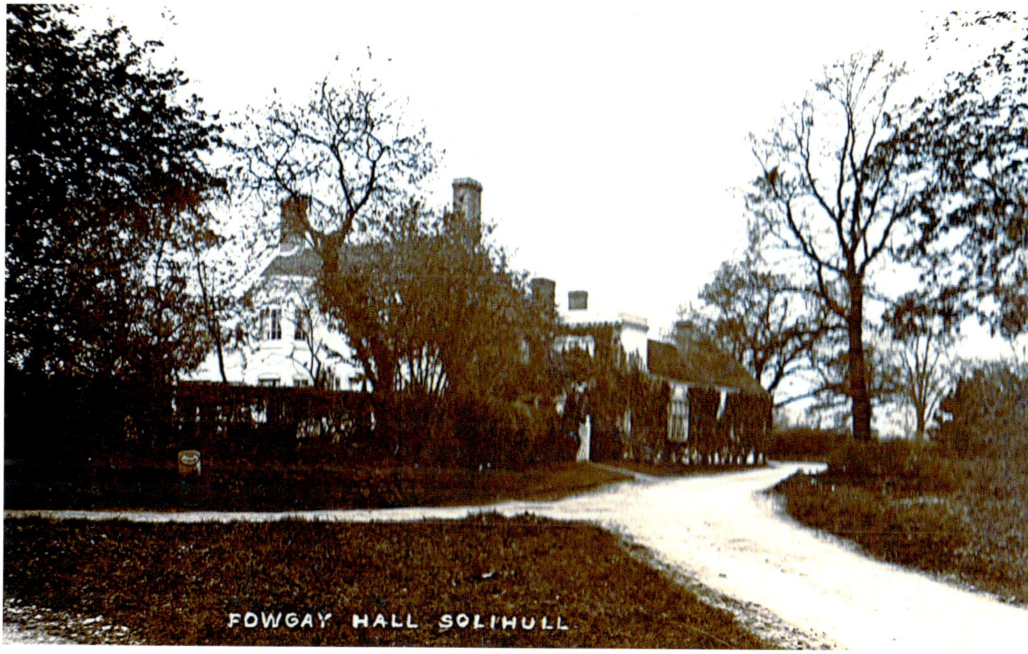

Fowgay Hall from the lane just before the First World War, from a postcard. (James Darwin)

private house. In 2006 Solihull Council refused consent to demolition but later lost on appeal through prompting by the Office of the Deputy Prime Minister (Lord Prescott), despite its Grade II listing. It was demolished – to be replaced by flats in an unlovely brick building mockingly bearing the same name – in 2007.

98. The Hill, Amblecote, Staffordshire. 2007

Amblecote passed from the Staffords to the Greys of Enville in the fifteenth century and the latter were still there in 1696 when the parish was becoming the centre of the glass-making industry. Paul Rogers of Wassell Grove (q.v.) entered business there and his son, Thomas Rogers (d. 1775), built a 'spacious brick mansion' called The Hill. It was a substantial mid-eighteenth-century structure of red brick with stone dressings and a pedimented garden façade. The entrance front was of nine bays and two storeys with attics above the cornice, like Samuel Galton's Duddeston. The fenestration had rusticated stone lintels and there were quoins at the angles. The tetrastyle Tuscan portico was added in the Regency period. Rogers was succeeded by his son Thomas Rogers MP (1735–93) but his son Daniel (1761–1829) retired to Wassell Grove in the Regency period, selling to the Mills, also glass manufacturers. George Mills committed suicide here in 1885, leaving massive debts. The mansion was then purchased and donated by John Corbett of Chateau Impney (Worcestershire) to the people of Stourbridge in 1891 as the site for a new hospital. The building was converted and opened in 1893, being later named the Corbett Hospital. It was considerably altered and extended, having large additions of the early 1970s attached to its garden front. In 2007, however, it was demolished, unlamented, and entirely replaced by modern buildings.

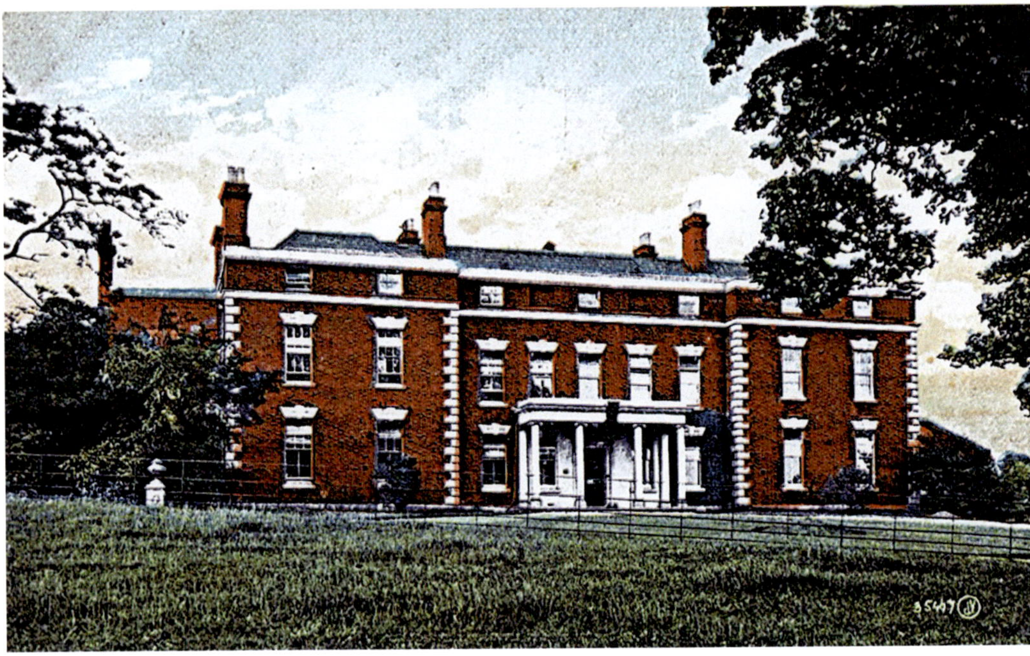

The Hill as a hospital, from a postcard of *c*. 1914. (James Darwin)